Here's one I made earlier

Scripture Union
craft resources for
3s to 11s

Kathryn Copsey

Scripture Union
130 City Road London EC1V 2NJ

First published 1995

ISBN 0 86201 981 8

The craft ideas in this book have previously appeared in issues of *Learning Together with Under 5s*, *Learning Together with 5–7s*, *Learning Together with 7–11s*, *SALT: 3 to 4+*, *SALT: 5 to 7+* and *SALT: 8 to 10+*.

British Library Cataloguing-in-Publication Data. A catalogue record for this book is available from the British Library.

Designed by Tony Cantale Graphics
Most of the illustrations are by Anna Carpenter
Other artwork by Pauline Adams, Anne Anderson, Debbie Annesley, Paolo Baigent, Rachel Beckingham, Evelyn Huntingford, Julie Moores, Sheila Pigrem, Neil Pinchbeck and Elizabeth Turner
Cover photograph by Peter Shoesmith

Printed and bound in Great Britain by Ebenezer Baylis & Son Ltd, The Trinity Press, Worcester and London

Contents

Let's make ...

What images does the word 'craft' conjure up in your mind? A fraught leader surrounded by children clamouring for help while waving half-folded pieces of paper? Painty footprints on the floor, paste in little Sally's hair, and the look on Mrs Jones's face as she comes in to turn on the urn? Or perhaps you picture a small, industrious group of children with a leader, all well-covered in aprons, busy making thumb pots from playdough?

Some crafty rules

The thought of craft does not need to awaken in you a sense of dread. 'Making times' do not need to be chaotic, nor do you have to be an artist to do the activities in this book. A few basic rules can make craft sessions great fun and fill both you and the children with a great sense of accomplishment.

✔ **Practice** Make the craft item yourself beforehand so you are thoroughly familiar with it and know that it works. Bring samples to show. Make sure that it is easy enough to do with your group, or challenging enough to avoid the possibility of bored children stuffing *Blu-Tack* up the tap of Mrs Jones's urn!

✔ **Prepare** Make sure you have all the materials you need in a suitable form (eg, cut up, folded), and in suitable containers for the children to work with.

✔ **Protect** Make sure you have newspapers, aprons, polythene sheeting, soapy water, cloths, towels, kitchen towels and so on, available depending on what activity you are planning to do.

✔ **Divide** Work in small groups so that no children get frustrated while waiting for your help, and decide to pour paint into Mrs Jones's urn.

✔ **Delegate** Recruit one helper to each group. If you are short of help, prepare the activity to a stage at which the children need little or no help from a leader.

✔ **Decide** before the session what you are going to do with the finished products.

Wet items may be hung on a clothes horse or pegged to a line to dry (place newspapers underneath to catch drips, but make sure no picture will be spoilt by hanging it vertically while still wet – otherwise lay on newspaper or polythene sheeting on the floor). Models can be placed out of the way on trays to dry. Many pictures will look good mounted on contrasting sheets of coloured paper (eg, sugar paper). Friezes, collages, posters and pictures can be hung on a wall. Hang mobiles from a line until going-home time; laying them flat can have disastrous effects!

Above all, have ready-named labels or cocktail stick flags for identifying who the finished product belongs to. There is nothing more upsetting for a child (or a leader) than to discover that someone else has gone off with their precious creation.

Don't forget that while displaying craft items is fine, younger children especially love to take home and share their creations.

Your craft box

Keep a strong cardboard box well stocked with a supply of craft basics: paste and containers, spreaders, different sizes of felt-tipped markers (make sure they work!), pencils, rulers and rubbers, sticky tape (ideally with a dispenser – it lasts longer!), string, *Blu-Tack*, scissors (round-ended for the youngest, but do make sure they cut), a large pair of scissors for yourself, craft knife, hole punch, stapler and some spare staples.

Restock after each session, checking how much is in the paste pots. Ideally the box should have a lid. Stress that it is your box (decorate it as such!) – the children must come and ask you if they want anything from it. You may also like to have a box containing paints. Powder paints last longest and are very versatile, but if you do a lot of painting, you may like to keep some made up, or buy some ready-made.

Many suppliers sell paint pots, but here is a home-made version if you wish:

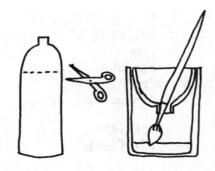

Cut off top of washing-up liquid bottle.

Remove cap. Turn top upside down and replace in bottle.

Cap can be replaced for storage of paint.

The value of craft

Creative activities have an enormous value in their own right as they provide a vehicle for children to express their imagination, skills, creativity, emotions, knowledge and potential. However, within a Christian context, whether it be a Sunday group, mid-week club, holiday club or whatever, they take on an even greater value. For if we believe that children are created in the image of God, then each creative activity a child makes or engages in is an expression of the gifts given by God to his children, and as such, a cause for giving him praise and glory.

As we look around his created world and marvel at the beauty, the greatness, the humour, the ingenuity, the variety displayed, so we can look at the 'creations' of our children and marvel at their wonderful inventiveness, imagination and skill.

By offering our children a wide range of activities at different ages, we provide the stimulus for their creative development which is all a part of helping them grow into whole human beings as God intended. As these activities can be used to explain or reinforce the Bible stories and themes we share with our children, we are helping them to grow also in their faith and their knowledge of God.

Let's make ...

There are sixteen sections in this book, each of which carries a short introduction highlighting a few points about the topic and detailing the contents. The final section features a number of useful templates which can be used in many of the suggestions.

Each section features a particular type of craft activity, eg, mobiles, clay, puppets. Then within each section you will generally find a number of different styles in which to make a given activity, followed by a number of topic approaches to the activity.

Most craft ideas are also followed by a paragraph entitled **USES**, which suggests ways in which the activity can be used, and the Bible passages and themes which can link with it. This is by no means exhaustive – the limit is your own imagination!

The crafts in this book are suitable across a wide range from around 3 to 11 years. It is expected that group leaders will know the potential and limitations of their children and will choose accordingly.

Finally, at the end of the book, you will find a topical index, alphabetically arranged. This should help to make the book a little more 'user-friendly'.

So, have fun! Try something you've never made before, think about how it can be adapted to link with your theme or the story you're about to tell, and ... happy making!

1 Let's make pictures

TWO-YEAR-OLD Cathi took a last big bite of boiled egg, turned over the shell in the egg-cup and pushed the plate towards her father. 'Daddy,' she announced, 'I want a man!' Her father smiled, picked up a pencil and proceeded to draw a funny face on the empty shell, much to Cathi's delight.

A little way down the road at play-group, her older brother, Simon, was busy making bright splodgy patterns all over a dark green sheet of card using shapes cut from potatoes and carrots. 'That's lovely,' said his play-group leader. 'I especially like the way you've mixed the yellow and the red together!'

Three miles away her oldest brother, Jeff, was working on a project about the French painter, Cézanne. 'I think the painting *The Card Players* shows a good use of tone,' he wrote. 'Cézanne uses lots of unusual colours and blends them all together well.'

Cathi, Simon and Jeff were all working with pictures, whether it was a pencil on an eggshell or oils on a canvas. As this section will show, the term 'pictures' covers an incredibly wide range of materials, styles and methods. Here you'll find pictures that use paint, wax, chalk, paste, sand. You'll find those that rely on light for effect, on wind, on colour, on pattern. And you'll discover that it is possible to use leaves, breath, bubbles, even ice to make pictures. Most of the ideas are very simple – often the skill lies in thinking up good ways of using the ideas and good ways of presenting the finished product. And who better to ask for creative ideas than the children themselves who draw such great enjoyment from experimenting with 'making pictures'?

The following styles and topics are covered:

USING PAINT
a Printing
b Dropper painting
c Spatter painting
d Bubble painting
e Blow painting
f Powder painting
g Finger-painting
h Splodge painting
i Wet paper painting
j Ice painting

MAKING PICTURES
a Drawing
b Sand pictures
c Wet chalk drawing
d Rubbings
e Wax pictures
f Embossed pictures
g Background pictures

SNOWFLAKES

STAINED-GLASS EFFECTS
a 'Stained-glass' pictures
b Candle pictures
c Window pictures

FINGERPRINTS

PAPER PEOPLE
a Zigzag people
b Cut-out people

WIND PICTURES

FISH PICTURES
a Magic fish
b Fish in the sea
c Goldfish tank
d Fancy fish
e Fish shapes

WEATHER PICTURE

DAY AND NIGHT PICTURES
a Day
b Sunset
c Night
d Day and night painting

MOSAIC PICTURES

USING PAINT

a Printing

• **Leaf prints** Make leaf prints by painting the back of the leaf, then pressing firmly on to a sheet of matt paper to reveal the shape and pattern of veins on the leaf.

• **Sponge printing** Cut shapes such as the moon and stars from pieces of sponge. Clip a clothes peg on to each one, then dip the shapes into a saucer of paint and print on to large sheets of paper.

• **Vegetable prints** Use pieces of carrot, potato, slices of peppers, and apple and pear halves. Dip the piece of vegetable into a saucer of fairly thick paint and print on to paper.

• **Miscellaneous prints** Have ready cotton reels, corks, card edges, doilies, string and so on, together with some different coloured 'printing pads': paper towel wads soaked in paint. Print pattern sequences based on shape or colour.

USES for printing: *Use to make borders, patterns, creation prints, themed collages, and so on. Make wrapping paper by printing a repeated pattern on a large sheet of paper, and make smaller similar gift tags.*

b Dropper painting

Provide clean medicine droppers and show children how to drop paint on to paper (using a different dropper in each colour). Experiment with dropping on to different types of paper: dry, wet, blotting paper, coffee filter paper, and so on.
USES: *Link with a theme on rain and how it falls to the ground.*

c Spatter painting

Provide old toothbrushes and show how to flick paint on to paper. (Older children will be able to run their thumbs across the bristles to achieve a fine, more even spatter.) Place a simple template shape on paper, then spatter. When the template is removed, an unpainted shape will be apparent on the paper.
USES: *Link again with a rain theme, or use to illustrate colour or pattern, or simply as a means of colouring in or decorating.*

d Bubble painting

Add a few drops of washing-up liquid to fairly thin paint, in an open-topped container. Blow down a straw until the coloured bubbles rise over the rim of the container. Place a sheet of paper over the bubbles and make a bubble print. (Practise blowing down a straw first as children are used to sucking straws!)
USES: *Use with a theme on colours and patterns in nature, or to decorate a poster or greetings card.*

e Blow painting

Drip a few drops of paint on to a piece of card, then move the paint along by blowing gently through a straw. For variety, dampen the card slightly before dropping the paint on it. Create and join trails of colours across the paper.

USES: *Link with a theme on wind – you cannot see what is pushing the paint across the paper; link with a Pentecost theme, thinking of how the good news about Jesus was spread.*

f Powder painting

Follow the directions given to show you how to do powder painting.

• **Pour a puddle of liquid starch or wallpaper paste on to paper. Spread with a brush.**

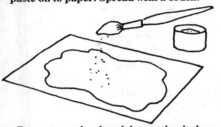

• **Prepare another brush by wetting it then dabbing dry with a cloth. With this brush, pick up paint powder and drop it on to the paper. Use several colours, then leave to dry.**

USES: *Use to decorate greetings cards, posters, and so on; link with themes on colour, patterns, texture and materials.*

g Finger-painting

In a saucepan, mix two tablespoons of cornflour with enough cold water to form a paste. Add about one cup of cold water and heat gently until the mixture reaches a custard consistency. Leave to cool then add dry powder paint.

Give children blobs of paint on a plain plastic tablecloth and let them 'draw' in it with their fingers. Afterwards, wash the cloth under running water.

Alternatively, use directly on a washable table or on paper. Simple finger-paints can be made by adding a few drops of food colouring to a flour and water paste although this does not dry as quickly, and can stain the fingers for a longer period.

USES: *Use specific colours or mix colours to link with a theme, eg, rainbow colours, colours used in the tent of meeting or the temple, colours in creation, and so on.*

h Splodge painting

Fold a piece of plain paper in half, then open out and drop large splodges of paint on one side only. Fold the paper in half again along the crease and press down, spreading the paint. Open up and talk about the resulting shapes. What do they look like? What changes have taken place?

USES: *Cut specific symmetrical shapes from paper, eg, a butterfly, a ladybird, geometric shapes, faces, and so on, and fold one half over so the same pattern is printed on the other side. Use with a colour or pattern theme, thinking of symmetry in God's world.*

i Wet paper painting

Provide sheets of damp paper by wiping the surface of the paper with a damp sponge just before painting. Pour small quantities of food colouring into saucers for the children to use as paint. This produces spectacular results.

USES: *Link with a theme on colour and patterns; use to decorate paper for wrapping paper.*

j Ice painting

Place a few colours of dry powder paint into shallow containers. Take blocks of ice and dip them into the paint and 'paint' with them on to paper. Use a different piece of ice in each colour.

USES: *Link with a theme on water (you may need to explain that ice is water) and its different uses; link with Bible stories to do with water or to do with God's provision of water.*

MAKING PICTURES

a Drawing

Let the children draw pictures of themselves on large sheets of paper using wax crayons. Have mirrors available, helping them to note length and colour of hair, clothes, eye colour, and so on. When completed, cut out in rough outline and arrange on a large sheet of paper so they clearly form one group.

b Sand pictures

Colour sand using vegetable food colouring and make some special pictures. Make sure the sand is dry, then paint thick paste over stiff coloured paper. Sprinkle sand over the paste, shaking off excess over newspaper. Frame or mount pictures and hang up.

c Wet chalk drawing

Beforehand, soak chalk in a mixture of sugar and water, then provide the children with damp chalks and dark paper and let them create their own pictures.

d Rubbings

Place a leaf, a coin, a piece of bark or wood under a piece of matt white paper. Rub over it gently with a wax crayon until the pattern can be clearly seen. Another option would be to go outside and make bark rubbings of different textures.

e Wax pictures

Draw patterns or pictures on white paper using a white wax candle or crayon. Paint over these with thin watery washes of bright or dark-coloured paint to reveal the pictures. Another option is to write secret messages in this way.

f Embossed pictures

Score the back of gold or silver wrapping paper with a ball-point pen or blunt pencil to produce a raised effect on the front. This can be done at random or, alternatively, draw around a template. When completed, embellish the design on the front by pasting on 'precious jewels' (shiny sweet papers). Cut out and frame or mount.

g Background pictures

Prepare outline pieces as shown for sea, rivers and hills, colouring them blue and green for the sea, blue for the rivers, and green and brown for the hills (use paints, crayons or

1. Colour top of large, background sheet blue (collage, paint or crayon). Add cotton wool clouds.

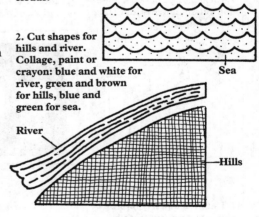

2. Cut shapes for hills and river. Collage, paint or crayon: blue and white for river, green and brown for hills, blue and green for sea.

River

Sea

Hills

3. Assemble on background.

paper collage). Assemble on a large background sheet and use as appropriate.

USES for making pictures: *Use these various approaches to making pictures to link with a variety of themes and Bible stories, and to provide the children with experiences of working with different types of materials to produce different effects.*

SNOWFLAKES

Fold circles of paper in half, then into thirds. Using scissors, snip pieces out of the folded circle to make snowflakes. Open out and note how each one is different.

Alternatively, cut them ahead of time and leave folded for the children to open and discover the interesting shapes. Younger children may find it easier to tear small shapes away instead.

These can be mounted on a dark background, hung as mobiles, or used as doilies when cooking is done.

USES: *Link with the theme that each of us is special and unique, just as no two snowflakes are the same; link with a theme to do with the beauty of creation.*

FINGERPRINTS

Make thumb- and fingerprints on plain paper. (Use either ink-pads or thin paints and have kitchen roll ready to wipe hands before washing.) Add more fingerprints and features to make people and animals as shown. Have the children write their names by the prints to show that each one is special. Try drawing an outline (eg, fish, owl or sheep) and let the children fill in the detail using finger and thumb-prints.

USES: *Link with the theme that each one of us is unique and special in God's eyes. Even our fingerprints are different to those of anyone else.*

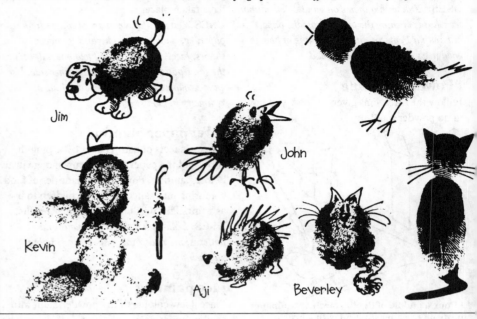

STAINED-GLASS EFFECTS

a 'Stained-glass' pictures

Make 'stained-glass' or 'see-through' pictures as shown. Younger children will find the pleat and notch approach easiest.

For younger children

• 'STAINED-GLASS' PICTURE

1. Pleat a piece of black paper and cut out notches and other small shapes.

3. Mount the finished picture on a piece of thin card.

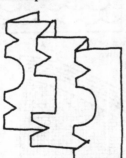

2. Unfold it and let children glue sweet wrappers, foil, cellophane, etc on the 'wrong' side to cover the holes.

• 'SEE-THROUGH' PICTURE

1. As 1. above.

2. Let the children glue coloured tissure paper and cellophane pieces at random on to grease-proof paper.

3. Cut to size of the pleated black paper and glue these two together.

For older children

Older children can cut out different shapes from the centre of a church window-shaped piece of black card to produce a leaded effect. The cut-out areas can then be pasted over with coloured tissue paper.

• 'LEADED' WINDOW

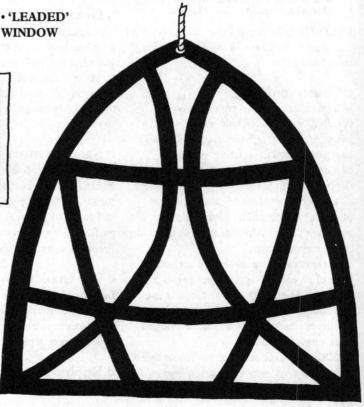

PAPER PEOPLE

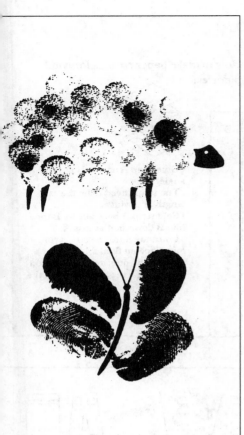

a Zigzag people

Fold a rectangle of paper concertina-style and draw a person on the top fold so that the hands and feet touch the side folds. Cut around the outline, leaving the hands and feet intact at the fold to produce a chain of zigzag people.

USES: *Link with a friendship theme; use to illustrate a crowd; use as a memory verse or theme phrase reminder by writing a word on each person; colour in the figures to represent a multi-racial group.*

b Cut-out people

Provide two large people shapes cut from stiff paper or card, and decorate the figures by pasting on an interesting selection of collage materials, eg, paper scraps, sawdust, ribbon, confetti, dried leaves or petals. Draw on faces. Tell the children they are making the figures into friends.

USES: *Use with a theme on friendship, talking about what makes a good friend and the things friends like to do together; link with the theme of Jesus as our friend.*

b Candle pictures

• **Design A** Cut out diamond shapes from rectangles of dark card, then cover the holes with pieces of coloured cellophane and add a flame at the top.

• **Design B** Provide candle shapes cut from brightly-coloured card which the children can decorate using gummed paper, shapes, cut-out motifs from wrapping paper, cards and so on.

c Window pictures

For younger children or if time is limited, fold a piece of card in half, draw one shape on it (eg, star or moon), cut through both thicknesses, paste a piece of yellow tissue paper inside the card and paste the two halves together. Hang up in the light.

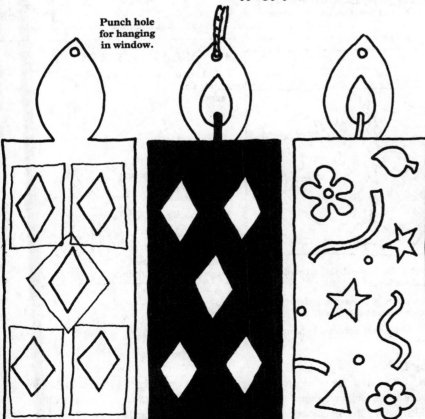

Punch hole for hanging in window.

USES for 'stained-glass' effect pictures: *Link with a theme on light, thinking about how light can make dull things beautiful and gives us colours. Link with Jesus as the light of the world; link also with a night-time theme.*

Design A (reverse)   Design A (front)   Design B (front)

WIND PICTURES

Make a series of pictures as shown, parts of which will move in a breeze, or when a hair dryer is blown across them. Some parts of the pictures could be mounted by means of a paper spring to allow movement (see instructions). Clouds, boats, etc, could be mounted on a separate strip of card which is slotted through the background at each end, then pulled along manually to show how the wind blows them along.

USES: *Link with a theme on the wind, on weather, on creation. Also link with a Pentecost theme, thinking about how the wind works and what it does.*

How to make paper springs for wind pictures:

- Glue strip A across B at right angle.
- The strips need to be the same length and width.
- Fold strip A back across B then fold B down and across A.
- Continue until the strips run out. Tape on final fold.
- When cut-outs are mounted on the springs, they will move in the 'breeze'!

- Mount kite on paper spring – blue background, cotton wool clouds.

- Make sails for windmill.

- Cut clothes separately. Glue or clip to a 'line' of wool. Tape wool behind picture.

- Leaves (tissue paper) glued to tree at one corner only. Mount boats on paper springs.

Cut-outs

FISH PICTURES

a Magic fish

Cut shapes of fish or other sea creatures from white matt card or paper then draw on a pattern using a white candle or white wax crayon. Let the children paint over them with bright, watery paint to reveal the patterns. Use in individual pictures, for a group collage or a mobile.

b Fish in the sea

Paint a large sheet of paper in watery blues and greens, allowing the colours to run and blend for effect. When this background is dry, paste on to it prepared fish shapes (including some seaweed, sea horses and shell shapes) cut from black paper.

c Goldfish tank

Make a goldfish 'tank' full of fish, as shown.

1. Give each child a 'tank' shape (made from card) to colour blue.

2. Let them paint or crayon fish shapes. Cut out and stick them in the 'tank'.

3. Cover in film or cellophane. Tape securely at the back.

d Fancy fish

Follow the directions in the picture to make decorative fish from coloured paper. Origami paper, which has a different colour on the reverse side, is particularly striking.

TO MAKE A FANCY FISH

1. Cut out a simple fish shape.

2. Fold in half and make angled cuts: longer in the middle, shorter on the outside.

3. Fold back each 'V' shape cut.

4. Mount on coloured paper and add a caption.

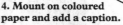

A fisherman called Peter followed Jesus. We can follow Jesus too!

Mount on paper of a contrasting colour, or hang in the window, or display with a caption on individual cards as illustrated.

WEATHER PICTURE

Using the weather templates from 'Let's make templates' (page 80), let the children compose their own weather pictures adding colour by using crayons, paint or felt-tips. Some children may prefer to draw their own pictures of fine or stormy weather from scratch.

USES: *Link with weather stories, eg, the storm on the lake, Noah's flood, the drought in Egypt, and so on.*

DAY AND NIGHT PICTURES

a Day

On a length of white or light blue paper, paste items to make a daytime picture, eg, sun, houses, flowers, birds feeding, trees, children playing. Draw these, cut from fabric or cut from magazines.

b Sunset

Paste strips of coloured tissue paper across a white paper background, or colour the background using red, orange, yellow, gold, pink, purple and pale blue to represent a sunset sky (as illustrated). Along the bottom, paste a selection of silhouettes of roof-tops, trees, mountains etc, cut from black paper. Add a semicircle of yellow card to represent the setting sun.

c Night

Make as for the sunset picture, but use overlapping strips of dark blue tissue paper, or blue, purple and black wax crayons. Add

silhouette shapes of roof-tops, trees and hills (as illustrated). Small yellow squares could be added to some of the houses to represent lighted windows. Add a moon and stars cut from silver and gold card, shiny paper, or foil.

d Day and night painting

Allow the children to experiment by painting with dark and light colours, giving them the opportunity to think about what represents day and night for them.

USES for day and night pictures: *Link with day and night stories, eg, Nicodemus coming to Jesus at night, the garden arrest, the pillars of cloud and fire, and so on; link with a creation theme.*

MOSAIC PICTURES

Write words in outline lettering or draw a pattern or picture on a large sheet of paper. Let the children fill in the shapes with small pieces of coloured paper torn from magazines to look like a mosaic. When colouring in a picture, make the colours appropriate to the shape being filled in, eg, grass should be filled in with green pieces of paper. Be sure to paste the background, not the individual pieces of paper.

USES: *Link with any theme. Even very young children can participate in this activity and the finished result can be very effective.*

SUNSET PICTURE   **NIGHT SKY PICTURE**

e Fish shapes

Experiment with one of the three approaches to decorating fish, illustrated in the accompanying diagram.

USES for fish pictures: *Link with any fish stories from the Bible, eg, the big haul of fishes, breakfast on the beach, and so on.*

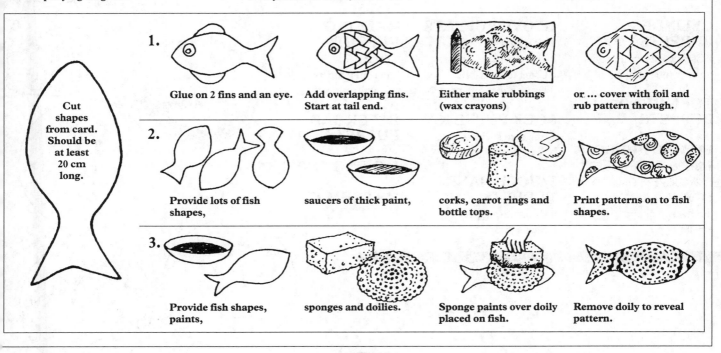

Cut shapes from card. Should be at least 20 cm long.

1. Glue on 2 fins and an eye. | Add overlapping fins. Start at tail end. | Either make rubbings (wax crayons) | or … cover with foil and rub pattern through.

2. Provide lots of fish shapes, | saucers of thick paint, | corks, carrot rings and bottle tops. | Print patterns on to fish shapes.

3. Provide fish shapes, paints, | sponges and doilies. | Sponge paints over doily placed on fish. | Remove doily to reveal pattern.

2 Let's make puppets

CYLINDER PUPPETS

a Cardboard tube puppets

Use sections of cardboard tubes, fabric or paper, and faces such as those shown to make small cylinder puppets. Paste fabric or paper around the lower half of each cylinder, then paste the face on the top half. Make a headdress from a small square of fabric and tie around the 'head' with wool. Cotton wool, wool or furry fabric could replace the headdress as hair.

USES: *These can be used as puppets by putting two or three fingers into the bottom of the tube to animate them. They can also be used as models in a story scene. They are simple for children to make – provide paper circles for them to draw their own faces.*

HAVE you ever watched a child's face while she is absorbed in a puppet show? Have you seen the concentration, the total involvement in the story? Puppets are a great favourite because children have such wonderful imagination. Sit two children down with a couple of puppets and you will discover that as they speak through the puppets, they become less inhibited, and their ability to express themselves and to build wonderful story-worlds is greatly enhanced. Puppets can add a great deal to the telling of a story, rhyme or song. They enable the storyteller to 'become' the character and to ask questions of the children directly, which helps to draw them into the activity.

Puppets don't need to be elaborate or expensive. Group leaders often shy away from using puppets because they think they are too difficult to make, or are the domain of 'proper' storytellers. But this is not so. A face on a cardboard tube or red lips and two eyes painted on a thumb and forefinger are enough to capture a child's interest and attention. And puppets are a good way of 'hiding' as a storyteller because the children are actually listening to the puppet and not to you. Of course, you need to be familiar enough with the story to tell it without notes and to make it come alive. But try it in front of a mirror; you'll discover you get absorbed in watching your own puppet!

Because a child's lively imagination can make a puppet so 'real', younger children can sometimes be a little fearful of a puppet and reluctant to engage with it. Don't move the puppet close to the child in such situations. Rather have the puppet chat to another child or to you, saying how much they want to be friends and asking them to pass on the message to the frightened child and so on.

So experiment with your puppeteering skills – try making some of these puppet styles – they can all be found on the next few pages.

• **Collect cardboard cylinders. Cover the lower half of each one with a different fabric.**

• **Draw different faces to stick above the fabric. Complete with headdresses tied around puppet with wool or string.**

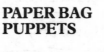

b Paper tube puppets

Make a quick and easy version of cardboard tube puppets by simply drawing a face on a small strip of paper, winding it around the finger and securing with sticky tape.

USES: *Use as a simple means of telling a story. These can also be made very easily by the children, but give assistance as to where to position the face and where to tape.*

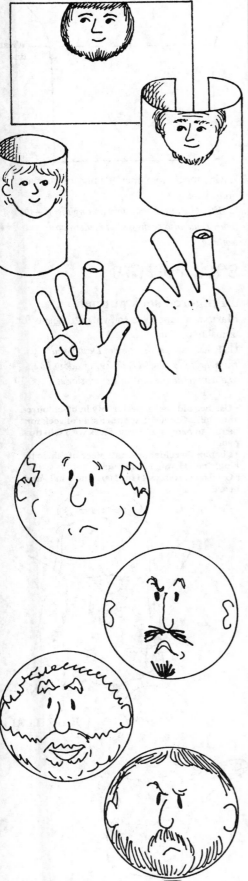

TUBE HEAD PUPPETS

Make puppets as shown using cardboard tube sections and pieces of material. Place hand inside and hold on to material to manipulate, or use a length of thin garden cane pushed up through neck and into the tube.

USES: *These are quite simple to make, and if not decorated further, can be used for either modern day or Bible stories.*

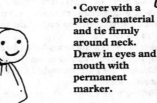

- **Cut a section from a cardboard tube for the head.**

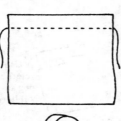

- **Cover with a piece of material and tie firmly around neck. Draw in eyes and mouth with permanent marker.**

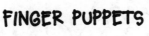

- **Make running stitches with strong cotton along one edge of sufficiently large piece of material. Leave thread loose at both ends.**

- **Slip around head. Draw ends firmly and tie at the neck.**

c Card puppets

Make finger puppets from card as shown below. Children can be involved in making these. Place the finger downward into the ring for ease of manoeuvring.

USES: *Include the children in the story by involving their puppets, eg, as members of Jacob's family, as part of a crowd listening to Jesus, as the disciples.*

CHILD. Draw a figure on to a thin cardboard shape about 8 cm long by 5 cm wide. Use bright or deep colours.

ADULT. Make rings of cardboard to fit loosely around children's fingers. Glue one to the back of each puppet.

d Fingertip puppets

Let the children draw faces on small, circular gummed labels and stick them to their fingernails.

USES: *Let the children talk to each other through their puppets, perhaps talking about the story or the theme of the session.*

FINGER PUPPETS

a Rubber glove puppets

Cut the fingers from rubber gloves of differing sizes. Draw features on the puppets using different coloured permanent pens, and/or decorate with collage materials, eg, wool, paper, cotton wool, using PVA glue.

USES: *Children can make animal puppets with these. They can also be made into people and used in telling a story.*

b Woollen glove puppets

Cut three fingers from a cloth or woollen glove (turn in or bind the bottom of the woollen glove fingers so they do not unravel). Sew or glue on features to make the three characters shown here.

USES: *Use to tell a story, making more puppets and changing the names as necessary.*

WOOLLEN GLOVE PUPPETS

— Fabric headdress

Wool for hair

Sequins, buttons or felt features

Fabric scraps in different colours

Cotton wool

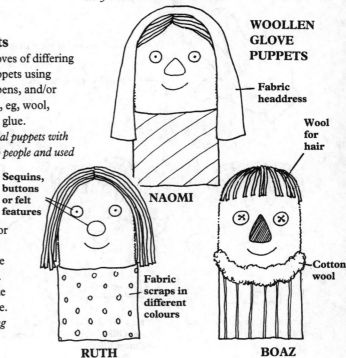

NAOMI

RUTH

BOAZ

e Felt puppets

Make the puppets as shown, again involving the children in the making.

USES: *Use as for the card puppets above, by involving all the children and their puppets.*

ADULT. In advance, cut pieces of felt 6 cm long by 4 cm wide. Trim to round-off upper edges. Place two pieces together and sew a zigzag stitch around the edge, leaving the lower edge only.

CHILD. Make the puppet character by glueing on fabric scraps, sequins, lace, small buttons, wool, etc.

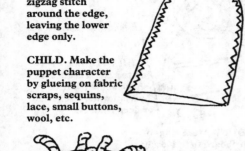

GLOVE PUPPETS

a Using gloves

Follow the directions to make a puppet from a five-fingered glove.

USES: *Use in telling a story in which the puppets do not need to look like Bible characters. Invite the children to bring in old gloves and make their own, then talk to each other. Link with a theme on communication or on caring for others.*

b Using paper

Make paper glove puppets as shown on the facing page.

USES: *Use with the story of Mary and the angel, or make additional puppets, dress them differently and use to tell another story.*

c Using felt or fabric

Make a basic puppet shape as shown, then adapt to make different characters.

USES: *Use with the story of Samuel or use the puppets to represent different characters, making additional ones from the basic shape as required. Practise the actions as shown.*

• On a piece of paper, draw around your hand (middle three fingers together, small finger and thumb stretched out). Add an allowance of 1 cm all round.
• Adapt this shape to make a pattern for a basic puppet shape – as shown on the right.
• Cut out the pattern and pin it to folded felt or fabric. Cut out.
• Sew or glue the two shapes together, leaving the bottom edge open. Decorate as shown on page 14.

BABY SAMUEL

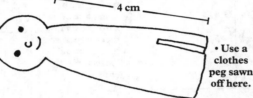

4 cm

• Use a clothes peg sawn off here.

• Draw features with felt-tipped pens – clothe in lint or white fabric.

d Using paper or fabric

Use card, fabric or felt and draw around your hand to make a figure, adding a generous allowance for joining. Paste or stitch together,

BASIC SHAPE

Glue on pieces of beige felt for face and hands.

Wrist line

leaving the bottom open. Paint, draw or paste on features.

USES: *Use in telling a story on any theme – the figure could also be dressed in modern day clothing.*

SOCK PUPPETS

a Fingered sock puppets

Make sock puppets as shown, cutting slits for 'arms' to protrude.

USES: *Use to tell the story of David and Barzillai (2 Samuel 17:27-29) or adapt faces and features to use in telling other stories.*

• Use two old socks, preferably light-coloured and plain. Cut a slit at either side of sock for 'arms' to protrude. Draw faces with felt-tip pens.
• Fix handkerchief or small piece of fabric to king's head using elastic band.
• Glue on cotton wool for Barzillai's hair and beard.

KING

BARZILLAI

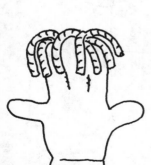

1. Take a five-fingered glove which fits you.

2. Sew the middle three fingers together.

3. Fasten strips of wool (or similar) for hair.

4. Sew buttons for eyes and nose. Glue felt or fabric shape for mouth.

5. Wrap a piece of cloth around back and arms.

b Simple sock puppets

Make simple puppets using an old sock, two buttons for eyes, and wool, felt, cotton wool, etc for other features.

USES: *Use to illustrate that the puppet is a lifeless old piece of material without a person's* hand in it, to make it do and say different things. *In the same way, the widow's son (or Lazarus, or Jairus' daughter) was a lifeless shell until Jesus commanded him to get up, and he became a living, breathing person again.*

PAPER GLOVE PUPPET

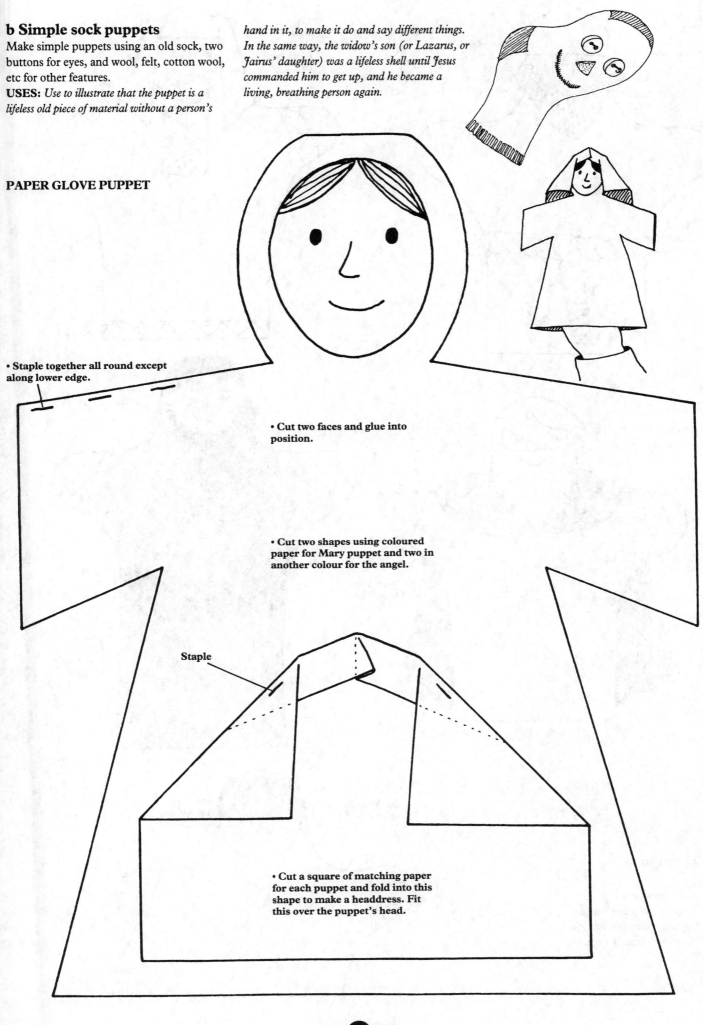

• Staple together all round except along lower edge.

• Cut two faces and glue into position.

• Cut two shapes using coloured paper for Mary puppet and two in another colour for the angel.

Staple

• Cut a square of matching paper for each puppet and fold into this shape to make a headdress. Fit this over the puppet's head.

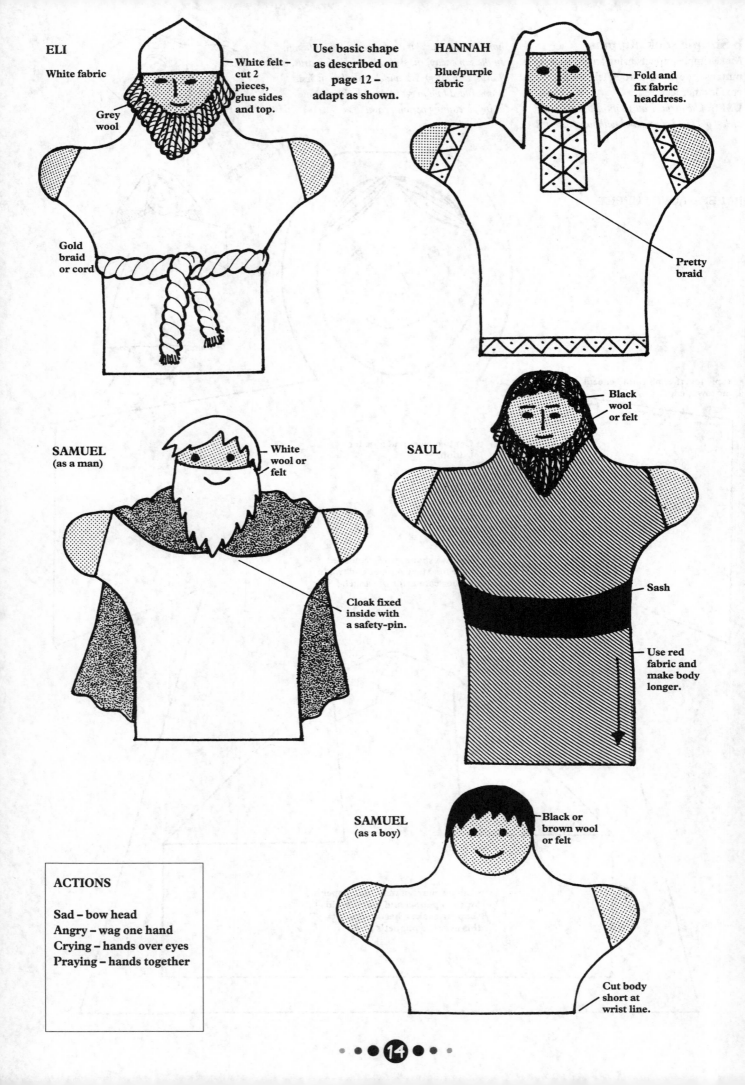

ELI

White fabric

White felt – cut 2 pieces, glue sides and top.

Grey wool

Gold braid or cord

Use basic shape as described on page 12 – adapt as shown.

HANNAH

Blue/purple fabric

Fold and fix fabric headdress.

Pretty braid

SAMUEL (as a man)

White wool or felt

Cloak fixed inside with a safety-pin.

SAUL

Black wool or felt

Sash

Use red fabric and make body longer.

SAMUEL (as a boy)

Black or brown wool or felt

Cut body short at wrist line.

ACTIONS

Sad – bow head
Angry – wag one hand
Crying – hands over eyes
Praying – hands together

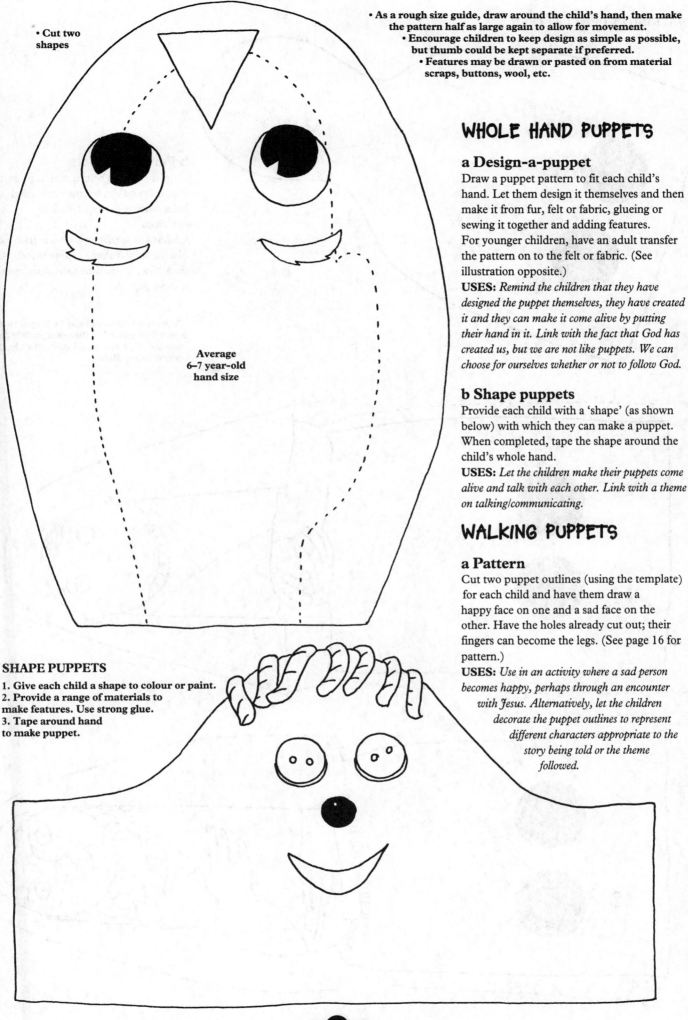

• Cut two
shapes

• As a rough size guide, draw around the child's hand, then make
the pattern half as large again to allow for movement.
• Encourage children to keep design as simple as possible,
but thumb could be kept separate if preferred.
• Features may be drawn or pasted on from material
scraps, buttons, wool, etc.

Average
6–7 year-old
hand size

WHOLE HAND PUPPETS

a Design-a-puppet

Draw a puppet pattern to fit each child's
hand. Let them design it themselves and then
make it from fur, felt or fabric, glueing or
sewing it together and adding features.
For younger children, have an adult transfer
the pattern on to the felt or fabric. (See
illustration opposite.)

USES: *Remind the children that they have
designed the puppet themselves, they have created
it and they can make it come alive by putting
their hand in it. Link with the fact that God has
created us, but we are not like puppets. We can
choose for ourselves whether or not to follow God.*

b Shape puppets

Provide each child with a 'shape' (as shown
below) with which they can make a puppet.
When completed, tape the shape around the
child's whole hand.

USES: *Let the children make their puppets come
alive and talk with each other. Link with a theme
on talking/communicating.*

WALKING PUPPETS

a Pattern

Cut two puppet outlines (using the template)
for each child and have them draw a
happy face on one and a sad face on the
other. Have the holes already cut out; their
fingers can become the legs. (See page 16 for
pattern.)

USES: *Use in an activity where a sad person
becomes happy, perhaps through an encounter
with Jesus. Alternatively, let the children
decorate the puppet outlines to represent
different characters appropriate to the
story being told or the theme
followed.*

SHAPE PUPPETS

1. Give each child a shape to colour or paint.
2. Provide a range of materials to
make features. Use strong glue.
3. Tape around hand
to make puppet.

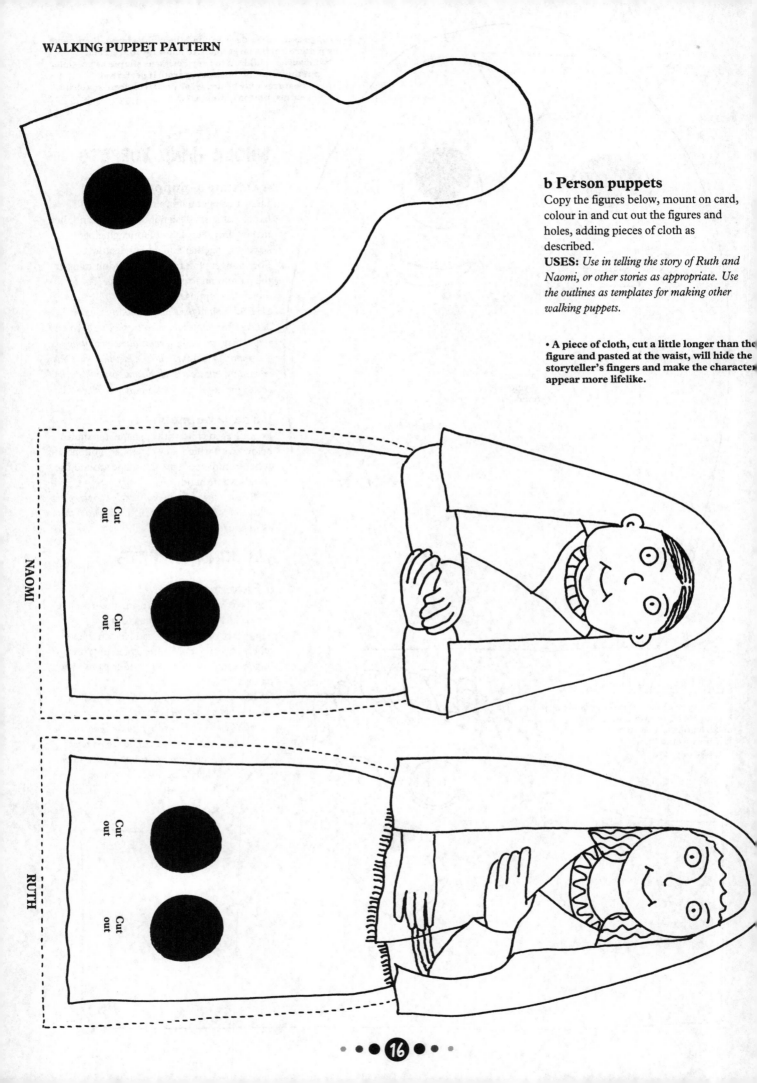

b Person puppets

Copy the figures below, mount on card, colour in and cut out the figures and holes, adding pieces of cloth as described.

USES: *Use in telling the story of Ruth and Naomi, or other stories as appropriate. Use the outlines as templates for making other walking puppets.*

• A piece of cloth, cut a little longer than the figure and pasted at the waist, will hide the storyteller's fingers and make the character appear more lifelike.

NAOMI

Cut out

Cut out

RUTH

Cut out

Cut out

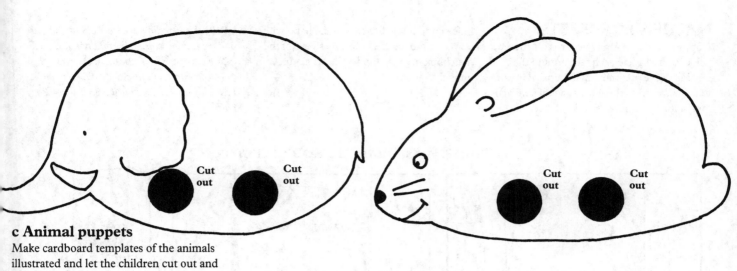

c Animal puppets

Make cardboard templates of the animals illustrated and let the children cut out and colour in their own animals.

USES: *Use with animal stories. Use in thinking about how animals use their legs; hopping, plodding, stalking, galloping, and so on; leading to thinking about how we use our legs.*

PAPER BAG PUPPETS

Make simple people or animal puppets from paper bags as illustrated; drawing on the face and pasting on additional features such as wool for hair, ears, etc. A paper bag with a separate base makes a good talking puppet; fold fingers over into base and move up and down.

USES: *Use in telling stories, or have the children create their own characters and make up their own stories.*

Talking puppet

• Use a gussetted paper bag with flat base.

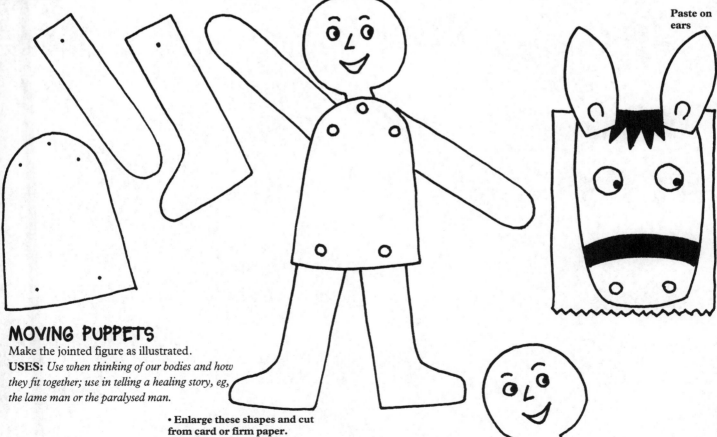

Paste on ears

MOVING PUPPETS

Make the jointed figure as illustrated.

USES: *Use when thinking of our bodies and how they fit together; use in telling a healing story, eg, the lame man or the paralysed man.*

• **Enlarge these shapes and cut from card or firm paper.**
• **Join with paper fasteners.**

MATCHBOX PUPPETS

Copy or photocopy the two faces illustrated, colour in and paste each face around the outside sleeve of a small matchbox. (Cut and fold cardboard to the same shape if sufficient matchboxes are not available.) Cover the index and middle fingers of each hand with a scarf or handkerchief. Slot the sleeve of the matchbox over the top to make a simple puppet.

USES: *Use in telling the story of the Pharisee and the tax collector; make additional faces for telling other stories. These are small puppets, so photocopy sufficient faces for children to make their own puppets and retell the story to each other.*

THE PHARISEE AND THE TAX COLLECTOR

3 Let's make cards

Thinking of you

USES: *On the inside write, 'Lord, help me to reflect you in my life', or 'Lord, help me to be like you on the inside', or a similar thought, and let the children take them home as reminders of the session.*

b Variety cards

Use a piece of thin card and design a card following the illustration. Care needs to be taken that children do not cut the 'frame' of the picture.
USES: *This method can be used to make cards for any occasion, linking with any theme.*

1. Take a rectangle of thin card and draw a simple picture on the front.
2. Carefully cut around the outline of the top half of the picture.
3. Then fold back the rest of the card. Don't forget to add a greeting at the bottom!
4. Use the same method to make a variety of cards.

Fold

Welcome!

New Home

Get Well Soon

Thinking of you

FOLD a piece of card or stiff paper in half and you have in front of you the basis for making one of 101 different designs of card. A pair of scissors will help you decide whether you want a shaped card, a stand-up card, a fan card, a pop-up card, a cut-out card ... Then you can draw, paint, paste, print, fold, cut, tear ... And the design you choose will depend on what and who it's for: a celebration card (Easter, Christmas, birthday), a get well card, a reminder card, a friendship card, a prayer card, a greetings card ...

A card doesn't need to be difficult to make in order to look impressive and to make an attractive gift. Contrasting colours, the use of a paper doily here and there, a carefully placed fold, even some fingerprinting can all be managed by the youngest of children with immensely rewarding results. Don't stop with the specific ideas that follow ...

On the next few pages are a number of basic card styles which can be adapted for many different purposes, followed by card designs for use on specific occasions. You will find:

•BASIC CARD STYLES

STAND-UP CARDS
a Person card
b Variety cards

MOVEMENT CARDS
a Tractor card
b Owl card

POP-UP CARDS
a Folded paper pop-ups
b Spring pop-ups

FAN CARDS

FACE CARDS

•TOPIC CARDS

GET WELL CARDS
a Plaster card
b Doily cards
c Elephant cards
d Picture and pattern cards

GREETINGS CARDS
a Flower cards
b Stencil cards
c Collage cards
d Gift card

CARING CARDS
a To the family
b From the family

PROMISE CARD

PRAYER CARDS

CHRISTMAS CARDS
a Angel cards
b Star card
c Present card

EASTER CARDS
a 3-D card
b A simple greeting
c Pop-up Easter card
d Rising sun Easter card

● BASIC CARD STYLES

STAND-UP CARDS

a Person card
Fold a thick piece of paper or card in half and draw a person-shape on the front as illustrated. Cut out, then add clothes and features.

MOVEMENT CARDS

a Tractor card

Cut the tractor from red card. Cut the wheels (shown here with dotted lines) separately from dark-coloured card. Paste the tractor shape to the background card, then push paper fasteners through all three thicknesses of card so the wheels move freely.

b Owl card

Cut the owl shape and wings (as shown) from brown or white card. Paste on the beak, then the eye circles. Decorate the body with a pattern (triangular carrot prints, zigzag crayoning or ric-rac braid). Attach wings behind body with paper fasteners, then paste top and bottom of body to background card leaving centre free for wings to move. Add stars and moon.

USES of movement cards: *Use these as 'gift cards' to help the children keep in touch with people they don't see very often. They can also link with a 'travelling' or 'movement' theme.*

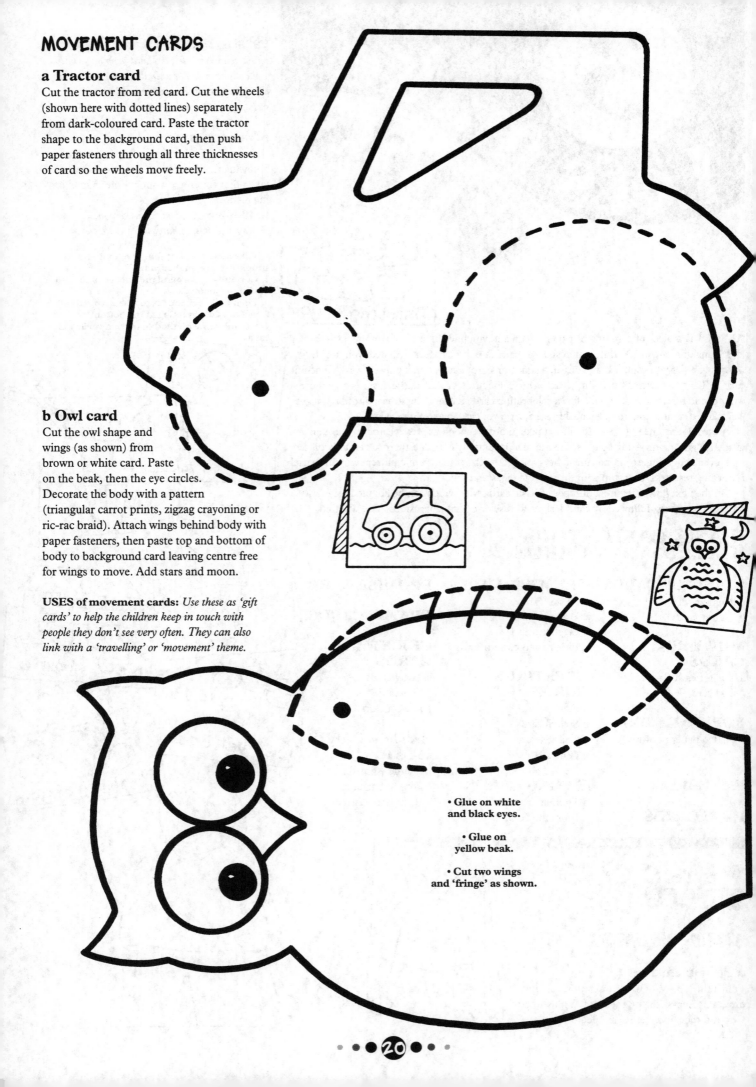

- Glue on white and black eyes.

- Glue on yellow beak.

- Cut two wings and 'fringe' as shown.

POP-UP CARDS

a Folded paper pop-ups

You will need two sheets of paper per card as well as scissors, paste and colouring materials. Follow the instructions on the diagram.

USES: *This illustration links with the story of Joseph, but could be used as a welcome/hello/celebration/invitation card.*

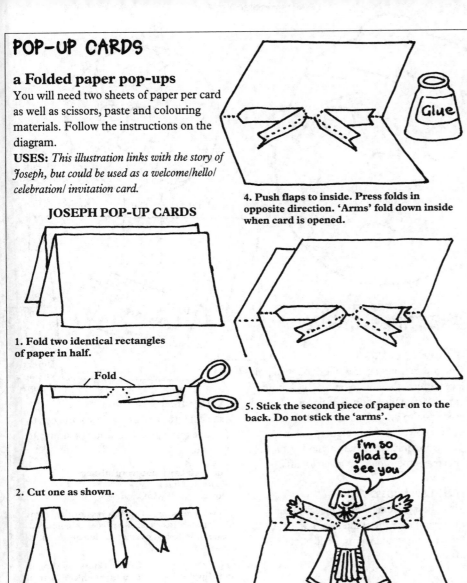

JOSEPH POP-UP CARDS

1. Fold two identical rectangles of paper in half.

Fold

2. Cut one as shown.

3. Fold flaps down.

4. Push flaps to inside. Press folds in opposite direction. 'Arms' fold down inside when card is opened.

5. Stick the second piece of paper on to the back. Do not stick the 'arms'.

I'm so glad to see you

6. Draw Joseph ready to hug Jacob. Stick on hands if you wish. Write what Joseph says and decorate front of card.

b Spring pop-ups

You will need a piece of card folded in half and pictures from an old greetings card. Follow the instructions on the diagram.

USES: *These can be used for someone who is ill, as a 'thinking of you' card for someone elderly or house-bound, or for a general greetings card.*

1. Stick picture from old card on the front. Cut out smaller picture for inside the card.

2. Fold strip of card concertina-style to make a spring.

3. Glue one end of 'spring' to page 3 of the card. Glue the other end to the small picture.

Get Well soon!

Love from

FAN CARDS

You will need a sheet of A4 paper for each card. Follow the instructions on the diagram.

USES: *The illustration links with the Easter story, the fan shape representing the rising sun, but any theme to do with celebration or surprise or joy could be used.*

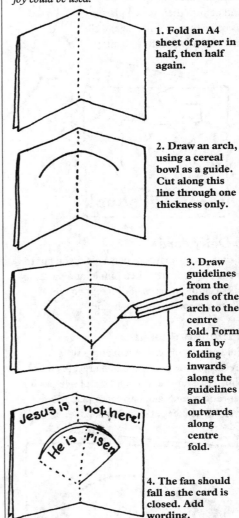

1. Fold an A4 sheet of paper in half, then half again.

2. Draw an arch, using a cereal bowl as a guide. Cut along this line through one thickness only.

3. Draw guidelines from the ends of the arch to the centre fold. Form a fan by folding inwards along the guidelines and outwards along centre fold.

Jesus is not here! He is risen

4. The fan should fall as the card is closed. Add wording.

FACE CARDS

Fold a piece of card or stiff paper in half and provide cut-out shapes of eyes, nose, mouth and ears for the children to arrange on the front of the card and make a 'happy face'. Write on each card a phrase such as, 'Have a happy day'.

USES: *Link with a family theme and give to family members. Use sad and happy faces for 'sorry' and 'thank you' prayer cards. Use to represent Bible characters and to take home as reminders of the session.*

● TOPIC CARDS

GET WELL CARDS

a Plaster card

Copy the face shown on to card and colour, then stick a plaster over the bump. Write a get well message inside before signing.

b Doily cards

Using small squares of paper, fold and cut to make paper doilies, then unfold and paste on to background cards of different colours. Write a get well message inside.

c Elephant card

Fold a piece of card in half and write a greeting at the bottom. Cut a grey, brown or pink circle for the head and simple shapes for ears and trunk, then paste into place. Draw eyes in black or cut from black paper.

d Picture and pattern cards

Cut out suitable pictures from birthday cards, magazines or flower catalogues and paste on to background card. You may like to cut around part of the picture, once it has been pasted on, to make a shaped card.

Alternatively, decorate the card with gummed paper shapes to make a pattern. Write a message on the front and/or inside.

Height of flower head 100 mm

Fold   Cut   Fold

Cut

Height of pot 110 mm

GREETINGS CARDS

a Flower cards

Cut circles from paper doilies, following the lacy pattern, then paste on to a background card to resemble a bunch of flowers. Use a green pen to draw the stalks and paste on a ribbon bow, cut from coloured paper. These are quick to make and look very effective – they could be given as gifts.

b Stencil cards

Make flower stencils from pieces of card, then paint over the stencils and draw in flower centres and stems. Write a greeting inside.

c Collage cards

Draw a bold design, eg, large flower, on a piece of folded card. Put paste on the petals, then screw up small pieces of tissue paper and stick on. Colour in leaves and paste on a ribbon bow.

d Gift card

Make a flowerpot card as shown, to give to someone on a special occasion or simply to say hello.

• For each card, cut from stiff card:
a flowerpot base,
a flower shape with stem.

• Cover one side of the flower (not the stem) with glue. Stick on small pieces of coloured tissue, but do not overload. Repeat on the other side.

• Fold the pot base. Cut two slots (as shown) and slip the flower stem through the central slot.

• Make a gift card to slip into the lower slot. Place a loop of tape behind to hold it in place.

CARING CARDS

a To the family

Make a card for the children to give to someone in their family to show a practical way in which they can demonstrate their caring. Use a postcard or folded card. Decorate the front or paste on a picture and, inside, write who it is for and what they will try to do to help in the week, eg, 'Dear Mum, I will try to keep my room tidy this week, Love from James'.

b From the family

As a response to the above, or as a separate activity, make help cards (as illustrated) for the parents or carers to fill in at home.

HELP CARD

Child's name

---------- has
helped at home
this week by

USES for caring cards:
These cards can be used to follow up the theme of encouraging the children to help and follow Jesus' example.

Decoration cut from a greetings card.

Parent to write down how the child has helped.

PROMISE CARD

Prepare some unfolded cards, postcard size or larger, and write on them one of God's promises, eg, 'God said, "I will be with you"', Genesis 28:15. Let the children add a decorative border and take them home to hang up as a reminder.

PRAYER CARDS

Provide geometrical shapes (circles, squares, hexagons) and print or crayon freely on these, then paste on to background cards. On the front write, 'God listens when we pray'. Fill in details inside as shown:

USES: *Send these to someone your child or your group has specifically prayed for. Select prayer needs to which the children can easily relate, eg, moving house, new baby, changing school, illness.*

EASTER CARDS

a 3-D card

Using the leaf template as shown, cut out a piece of green felt and a piece of thin card. Paste together, then paste the tips of the leaves only on to the background card, so that the leaf section lies slightly raised in the centre. Using the petal template and coloured felt, paste the petals to the centre of the leaves. Decorate as desired and add a greeting.

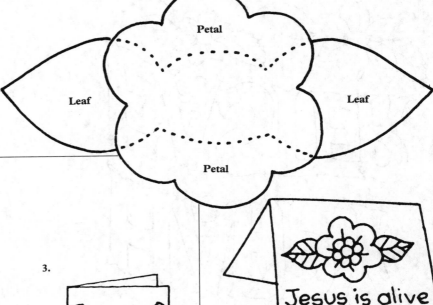

b A simple greeting

Prepare rectangles of card as shown. Slot the stalk of a fresh flower or piece of foliage through slit and tape at the back.

CHRISTMAS CARDS

a Angel cards

Follow the directions on the diagram to make these simple but impressive-looking cards.

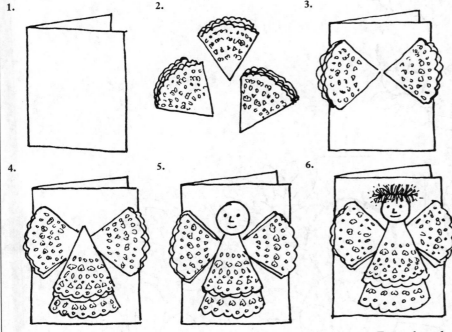

b Star card

Paste a black circle on to the centre of a red background card, then on the circle paste a star made from silver foil.

c Present card

Fold a piece of card into a rectangle, then fingerprint inside the outline lettering of 'Jesus' as shown. Sprinkle glitter down the sides. Inside write, 'has been born', then attach a ribbon to the back and tie at the front in a bow.

For each card you will need: a piece of card, paper doilies, a circle of paper (head), a short length of tinsel, glue-stick.

c Pop-up Easter card

Photocopy the master card below and colour it in, then fold the card in four. Cut along the bold lines at the top and bottom of the daisy and ease forward, folding along the dotted lines and making a crease down the centre of the daisy. The daisy will 'pop out' each time the card is opened.

d Rising sun Easter card

Photocopy the master card on the facing page, having cut off and separately photocopied the directions. Colour in the card and the sun and follow the directions for making.

To ....
From ....

'The Lord is risen indeed'
Luke 24:34

Jesus is alive!

On this Easter Day

How to make:

1. Cut neat slits along the two bold straight lines inside the card.
2. Fold card in half, then in half again along dotted lines (slits are inside).
3. Colour card and sun.
4. Cut out sun and strip.
5. Fold up flap on strip and insert in card from inside, so that 'pull' shows at top right-hand corner slit and flap protrudes from bottom long slit.
6. Paste sun on protruding flap.
7. Pull tab and watch sun rise.

Cut slits

Pull tab

Insert here

Paste sun to tab

Folded strip to insert into card

Fold up

Flap

Cut out strip

PULL

Sun (cut out)

4 Let's make music

b Box, bottle and tin shakers
Use any household containers with sealable lids, eg, plastic bottles, tins with plastic lids, cereal boxes, flat cheese boxes, *Smartie* tubes – thoroughly cleaned and dried. Soak the labels off clear bottles – the children will enjoy seeing the contents as they play. Paint other bottles with plain PVA paint, and cover boxes and tins with decorative sticky-backed plastic. Decorate with coloured stickers, sticky shapes or paper streamers. Fill with dry sand, large beans, pasta shapes, gravel. Tape up securely. NB Do not use uncooked kidney beans as these are poisonous.

c Coat-hanger shaker
Make several 'necklaces' of milk bottle tops, pieces of crisp packets, pasta, etc. Tie them to a wire coat-hanger and shake gently.

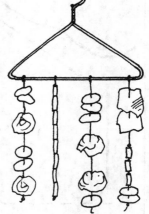

d Balloon shakers
Put some large, dried beans (not small beans or pulses and not kidney beans) into a balloon, then have an adult blow it up and tie it. These can be decorated with stickers or spirit-based markers.

e Simple maracas
Put scrunched-up foil pieces into a strong paper bag and tape the mouth closed.

TAPPERS

a Yoghurt pot drums
Cut a circle of paper such as grease-proof paper to fit over the top of a yoghurt pot allowing plenty of overlap. Secure with a rubber band and encourage children to tap gently with their fingers. Catering tins prepared in a similar way also make good drums.

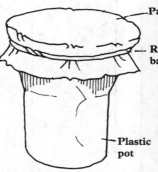

b Bottle xylophone
Fill different shaped bottles with different levels of water and tap with a stick.

SINGING good songs is fun.
Singing good songs, with actions, is even more fun.
Singing good songs, with actions, where the rhythm can be enhanced with percussive instruments is best of all!

This section suggests ways of making a wide variety of percussion instruments, from simple shakers to clay wind chimes. All of these can add a great deal to the enjoyment of a singing or worship time when used thoughtfully. Don't allow the tappers or blowers to drown out the pluckers. Plan different percussive effects to link with the words of a song. Choose some songs which focus on specific instruments to allow everyone to have a turn. Include an instrumental verse, so as to allow time to focus on words and actions in other verses.

Do you have children who really dislike singing? Involve them instrumentally. Do you have those who complain that they 'never get a turn'? Plan to change instruments after each verse of a song. Do the youngest children have problems with some of the words? Arrange a percussion solo just for them. Finally, make and decorate your instruments creatively – there is no need to advertise healthy eating yoghurt or liquid detergent! Enable the children to take pride in playing their instruments in a group – and there are lots to choose from.

RINGERS
a Percussion bells
b Tambourines
c Hand bells

SHAKERS
a Yoghurt pot shakers
b Box, bottle and tin shakers
c Coat-hanger shaker
d Balloon shakers
e Simple maracas

TAPPERS
a Yoghurt pot drums
b Bottle xylophone
c Chime bar
d Rhythm sticks
e Coconut clappers

BLOWERS
a Kazoo
b Trombone
c Trumpets

SCRAPERS
a Sandpaper scrapers
b Dowels

PLUCKERS
Harps

WIND CHIMES
a Foil
b Dough

RINGERS

a Percussion bells
Cut out a semicircle of stiff card – with a hole in the middle large enough to make a handhold – and colour both sides. Fasten three or four cheap bells (cat's collar bells) around the curved edge using wire twisters (eg, those supplied with plastic freezer/food bags).

b Tambourines
Attach small bells or milk bottle tops around the edges of strong paper plates or half of a flat round cheese box.

c Hand bells
Tie or plait cat bells into strands of wool or string, or pin bells to either end of a short piece of sanded dowelling rod.

SHAKERS

a Yoghurt pot shakers
Tip grains, pasta, lentils or beans into one pot, invert a second one on the top and tape securely as shown. Cover with sticky-backed plastic material to secure and to decorate. NB Do not use uncooked kidney beans as these are poisonous.

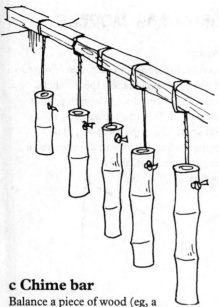

c Chime bar
Balance a piece of wood (eg, a length of 1 or 2 inch square) between two chairs. Using string, tie pieces of cut bamboo cane at intervals along the bar (thread string through small holes drilled in the cane). Tap canes with a stick.

d Rhythm sticks
Tap together two pieces of dowelling cut to the same length. These can be decorated with paints or felt-tips and coated (by an adult) with clear gloss enamel.

e Coconut clappers
Saw a coconut in half and remove flesh. Strike open ends together for a clip-clop sound. Decorate by pinning streamers to either end.

BLOWERS

a Kazoo
Wrap grease-proof or tracing paper over a comb and make a humming noise by blowing through it with the mouth touching the paper so that it vibrates.

b Trombone
Use cardboard tubes and a plastic pot to make a trombone as shown.

1. Find two tubes, one to fit inside the other.

2. Stick a plastic pot to the end of a third tube.

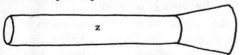

3. Wrap a paper strip around y and z and secure it with tape .

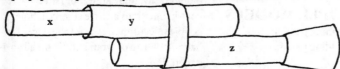

4. Slide x into y. Sing into x, while sliding the y/z unit up and down.

c Trumpets
Decorate semicircles of stiff paper, then roll to form a cone and staple or tape into shape as shown.

SCRAPERS

a Sandpaper scrapers
Tape or glue pieces of sandpaper to two blocks of wood and rub together.

b Dowels
Notch two lengths of dowelling at intervals as shown. Sand well and rub together.

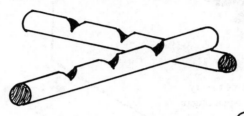

PLUCKERS

Harps
Use small, strong boxes with three or four rubber bands of different thicknesses to each box. Remove lids and have an adult cut small notches on either side of the box to hold the rubber bands. Settle the bands into the notches (as shown) and pluck. Experiment also with plastic punnets, foil cases and polystyrene trays. These are best used where they will not be drowned out by louder percussive sounds.

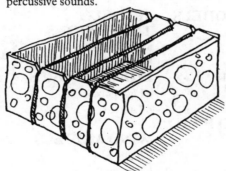

WIND CHIMES

a Foil
Thread flattened milk bottle tops or other foil lids on to lengths of wool and hang six from the six sections of a cardboard egg-box. Hang outside or where a breeze will catch it.

b Dough
Make a batch of baking dough following the recipe below, then roll out and cut shapes, ensuring that there is a small hole in each shape for hanging. (The hole will get smaller in the baking, so make sure it is large enough.) When baked and cooled, thread with string and hang together in the wind.

1. Make dough by mixing:
4 measures plain flour,
1 measure salt,
$1\frac{1}{2}$ measures warm water.

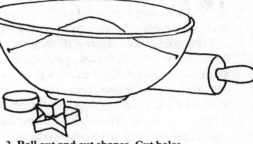

2. Roll out and cut shapes. Cut holes.

3. Bake shapes on a low heat. When cool, tie with string.

4. Hang together in the wind.

5 Let's make models

'MUM, I want to make something,' came the cry. 'Well, what about doing some finger-painting or making a pasta picture?' 'No,' emphatically. 'I want to make something that stands up.'

Perhaps this is a good way of distinguishing models from other forms of craft – they can usually stand up. In other words, they have a three-dimensional element. Children enjoy models for this reason – they seem to have a life of their own. You don't hang them on the wall, eat them or wear them. You can play with them, put things in them, use them, talk with them, give them as gifts.

There is no basic style for a model. You may be able to make different kinds of baskets, pigs or sheep, but basically each model 'stands on its own'. So in this section you will not find any basic model styles, but rather lots of specific models to make. You can choose one to link with your theme and Bible story. So whether you want ideas for Christmas or ways to illustrate an eastern home, the chances are you'll find something to meet your needs here. Try some of the following:

CHRISTMAS MODELS
a Stars
b Christmas tree
c Christmas wreath
d Angels
e New Year bells

FLOWER MODELS
a A pot of flowers
b A bunch of flowers
c Paper carnations
d Growing flower
e Say it with flowers

BOXES AND BASKETS
a Little boxes
b Giving box
c Tulip basket
d Envelope basket
e Sweet basket
f A huge basket

HOUSE MODELS
a Eastern houses
b Our home
c Card homes

ANIMAL MODELS
a Egg-box animals
b Pig faces
c Model pig
d Butterfly models
e Peacocks

BOATS AND FISH
a Fold-a-boat
b Sailing boat
c Boat on wheels!
d Handy fish
e Peter and us

SHEEP MODELS
a Jumping sheep
b Matchbox sheep
c Stand-up sheep
d Fridge magnet
e Cork sheep
f Card sheep

PALM BRANCHES
a Simple branches
b Pull-out branches

MODEL TELEVISIONS
a Simple televisions
b Cereal box television

LIGHT MODELS
a Lighthouse
b Lantern

WIND MODELS
a Balloons
b Windmills
c Kites

PICTURE FRAMES
a Hanging frame
b Standing frame
c Simple frame

MODEL TELEPHONES
a Simple telephones
b Yoghurt pot telephone
c Tin can phone

PEOPLE MODELS
a Spinning person
b Nodding person

CHRISTMAS MODELS

a Stars
• **Star decorations** Cut large stars from card and paste on pasta shapes: spirals, shells, wheels, etc. When dry, spray with gold or silver metallic paint and hang up.
• **3-D stars** Using the template, make hanging stars as shown and decorate them with glitter, sequins, shiny paper, etc.

• **For each star, cut out two shapes from shiny card or stiff paper.**
• **Cut along AB.**
• **Slot AB into AB to make a 3-D star.**
• **Decorate with glitter. Attach thread for hanging on tree.**

b Christmas tree
Cut two Christmas tree shapes from stiff green card. Slit one down the middle from the top to the centre, and slit the other from the bottom up to the centre. Decorate both sides of the trees (avoiding the slits) by painting on baubles or pasting on coloured shapes, glitter or wisps of cotton wool. When finished, slot one tree into the other to stand up.

c Christmas wreath
Make a basic shape from two large rings of corrugated cardboard stuck together (draw around two different sizes of plates and cut out with a Stanley knife), or bend a wire coat-hanger into a circle. Pierce a hole, a couple of centimetres from the edge, for hanging. Paste or wrap and tie on all sorts of decorations.

Make a nature wreath using pine cones,

green ribbons, dried leaves, seed pods, and so on.

Make a glittery wreath using tinsel, tree decorations, ribbons, and so on. Add a bow and thread through a ribbon for hanging.

d Angels

• **Lacy angels** Make angels as shown and hang as decorations.

For each angel you will need:
2 paper doilies,
Circle of foil or flattened milk top,
Circle of paper,
Stapler or glue.

1. Fold doilies in half.

2. Fold one again.

3. Draw face on circle of paper.

4. Glue face to foil or bottle top.

5. Glue head to body.

6. Glue second doily at the back.

NB Staples will hold the angel together better. This could be done to add strength after the children have glued the pieces together.

• **Hanging angels** Use the angel template to make card angels, decorating the wings with silver foil, glitter or sequins.

• For each angel cut out a circle (to the size shown) of white or silver card.
• Cut along solid lines. Fold along dotted lines.
• Staple or tape along line AB to CD.
• Attach thread to 'head' for hanging on tree.

e New Year bells

Make New Year bells as illustrated:

1. Prepare 4 small, disposable drinking cups (paper or plastic) by decorating them with ribbon, felt-tips, etc – writing on the year. (NB Spirit-based markers must be used on plastic.) Egg-box sections may also be used.

Pierce holes

2. Prepare 4 x 30 cm long pieces of wool, tying a large knot in the wool to keep the clapper in position when hung, and a small knot for the clapper.

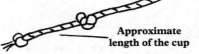

Approximate length of the cup

3. Prepare 4 x 10 cm square pieces of kitchen foil. Wrap the bright side of the foil around the lower knot. Squeeze into a ball to make clapper.

4. Thread the wool through the hole in the cup.

5. Tie the wool together leaving a hanging loop.

● The hardest part for the children will be tying the knots in the right places!

USES for Christmas models: *Link with any Christmas theme: the message of the angels, the wise men, offering a welcome as the shepherds welcomed Jesus, looking forward to the future with Jesus.*

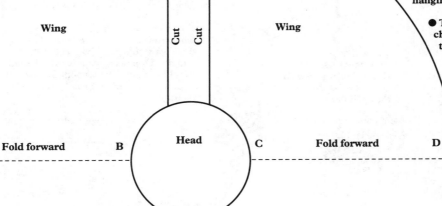

Wing — Cut — Cut — Wing

A — Fold forward — B — Head — C — Fold forward — D

Fold forward

Body

FLOWER MODELS

a A pot of flowers

Make simple but effective flower arrangements as shown:

For each flower arrangement you will need:

1 medium-sized pot, eg, yoghurt pot,

a small amount of *plaster of Paris*,

2 or 3 bendy straws and

crêpe or tissue paper (various colours).

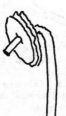

1. Cut paper into circles. Pierce each one with a pencil. Push about 10 circles on each straw. Scrunch up paper to make petal shapes.

2. Mix plaster and pour into pot. Arrange flowers.

3. Decorate with a bow if you wish.

b A bunch of flowers

Follow the illustration to make a bunch of flowers to give to a friend.

• **Cut 6 circles of coloured tissue paper and make a tiny slit in centre of each one.**

• **Thread stick or pipe cleaner through centre of petals using paste to secure.**

• **Attach ball of tin-foil to top of stick.**

• **Why not add some leaves attached with thin wire!**

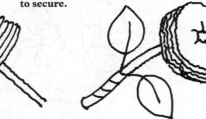

c Paper carnations

Make a basket full of carnations as shown (see basket pattern).

1. Cut tissue in half lengthwise.

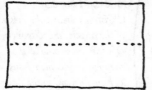

2. Place cut sides together.

Cut sides

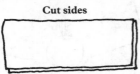

You will need:
Pink paper tissues,
Hair grips or paper clips,
Green florist's or insulating tape,
Pipe cleaners.

3. Fold concertina-style in 1.5 cm folds.

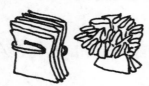

4. Pinch tissue across middle with hair grip or paper clip.

5. Fluff up portion above clip, pulling out several layers.

6. Insert pipe cleaner under clip. Wind tape around the tissue and pipe cleaner to make stem.
Carnations may be arranged in long 'baskets' made from envelopes.

d Growing flower

Use thick brown or red card for the pot and white card, which can be coloured on both sides, for the flower and stem (see illustration). Make the slit in the pot just large enough to catch the stem, and let the flower 'grow' as the children push it through.

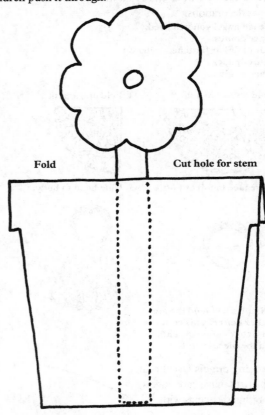

Fold   Cut hole for stem

e Say it with flowers

Make simple paper flowers as illustrated:

1. Cut 15 cm lengths of floral/garden wire and bend top over. Mould a small ball of plasticine over loop.

2. Cut out six circles of tissue paper. Fold each circle into six and cut edges rounded or pointed.

3. Paste centre of each circle thoroughly then thread onto wire. Twist and mould petals around plasticine.

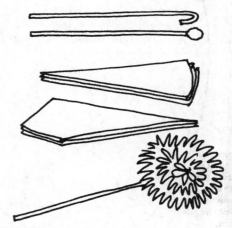

USES for flower models: *Link with themes to do with caring and giving as each of these flower models can be made and given as a gift; link also with Bible stories to do with friendship.*

BOXES AND BASKETS

a Little boxes

Make little boxes as shown in the illustration. You may need to practise several times.

USES: *These boxes are designed to be used as phylacteries, but can have any number of other uses also.*

1. Cut square from thin card (or greetings cards) or heavy paper. Fold into quarters, then open out.

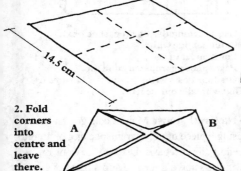

14.5 cm

2. Fold corners into centre and leave there.

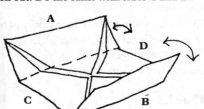

A   B

3. Fold opposite sides (A & B) into centre then open out. Do the same with sides C and D.

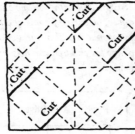

A
D
C   B

4. Open square completely and cut as shown.

Cut Cut Cut Cut Cut

b Giving box

Enlarge the outline illustrated to make a money-box, decorating the box as suggested, or pasting appropriate pictures on it.

USES: *As designed in the picture, use to encourage children to give money to those in need. The pictures could be changed to illustrate whatever project you are collecting for.*

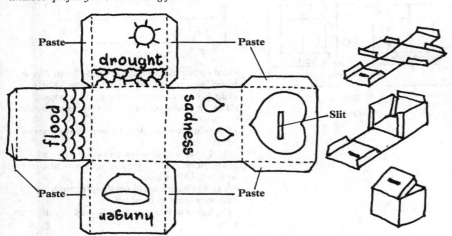

Paste — drought — Paste
flood
sadness
Slit
Paste — hunger — Paste

---

5. Make box by folding inwards along existing folds until sides A and B stand up to make square sides of box.

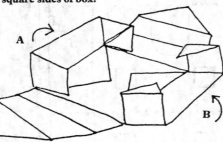

A
B

6. Now fold remaining sides inwards to secure. Cut square of card the size of the base of the box and push into bottom of box to hold flaps down.

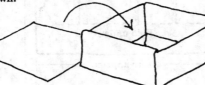

7. Make a second box from a square 0.5 cm smaller than the first square and slot into the

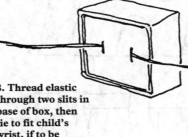

8. Thread elastic through two slits in base of box, then tie to fit child's wrist, if to be used as a phylactery.

Make a simple basket as shown and line with a doily.

USES: *This is an ideal size for holding a small gift (biscuits, flowers) and giving to someone. If made from large circles, it can be turned upside down and worn as a hat!*

1. Fold two circles in half.

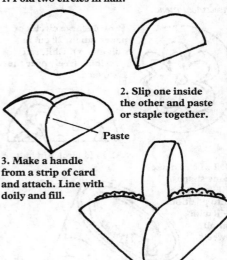

2. Slip one inside the other and paste or staple together.

Paste

3. Make a handle from a strip of card and attach. Line with doily and fill.

d Envelope basket

An incredibly simple but effective way to make a simple basket.

USES: *This is ideal for giving a small gift to someone.*

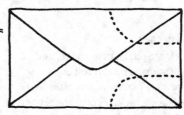

1. Seal an envelope.

2. Cut away shapes as shown.

3. Decorate with gummed shapes or crayons.

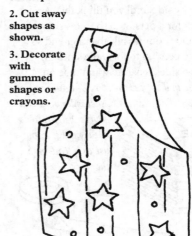

---

e Sweet basket

A simple but effective basket (see below). Another option is to paste a doily on to a circle of dark-coloured paper and twist into a cone. If the doily is slightly larger than the paper, a lacy border appears at the top of the cone.

USES: *A very attractive way to give a gift of sweets to a friend.*

1. Provide large circles of paper (about 20 cm in diameter). Children scribble freely over the surface.

2. Fold circles in half.

3. Twist to make cone shapes. Glue or tape into position. Fill with small sweets.

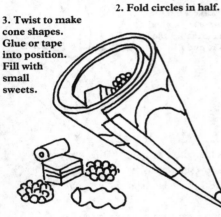

f A huge basket

Have ready a large pile of newspapers and several rolls of sticky tape and roll up individual sheets of newspaper to make long tubes. (Broadsheet newspapers are larger and therefore make longer tubes. Roll diagonally for greater length and strength.) Lay all the tubes side by side until you think the base is big enough for a person to sit in (as shown), then continue adding rolls to either end so they can be bent up to form the sides. Make the last two sides separately and tape on.

USES: *Use to illustrate the story of Paul's escape in the basket. The finished basket will not hold a child's weight, so do not try to lift it, but use as a lead-in to the story.*

HOUSE MODELS

a Eastern houses

• **Paper house** Make a simple but effective paper house as shown.

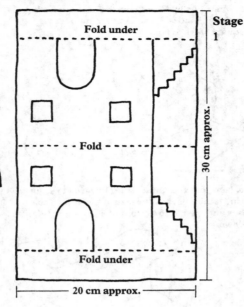

Stage 1

Fold under

Fold

Fold under

30 cm approx.

20 cm approx.

Stage 2

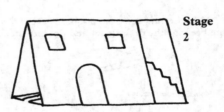

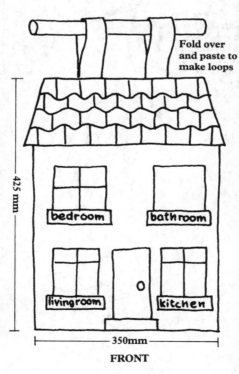

Fold over and paste to make loops

425 mm

bedroom   bathroom

livingroom   kitchen

350mm

FRONT

• **Model house** Make a house from a shoe box and decorate as shown. You could paste the lid on upside down to get the parapet effect on the roof.

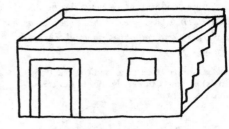

• Use a rectangular box (eg, shoe box).
• Paint outside white.
• Paint on features.
• Paste paper parapet around top.
• On door posts write, "Love the Lord your God with all your heart".

• **Nazareth house** Make a collage of a house using a piece of polystyrene packing or an old ceiling tile as a basis. Use pens to draw on windows and a door and add a flight of steps cut from white paper. Finish with a fabric tree, a sandpaper road and a sun cut from yellow card.

USES for house models: *These models can be used when talking about the homes people lived in, in New Testament times; link with 'house' stories such as the paralysed man.*

b Our home

Make a 'hanging home' as shown.

USES: *Link with a theme on our homes, on the family, on caring for one another. The windows can open to reveal pictures of people, messages as to how the children can help in these rooms, and so on.*

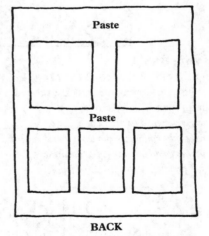

Paste

Paste

BACK

• Cut out front and back of house from *Vilene* (interfacing material available from fabric shops), heavy cloth or strong, thick paper. (If using *Vilene*, draw on it using spirit-based markers.)
• Cut windows and doors along heavy lines to open.
• Apply paste to shaded areas on back and paste on to front. Door and windows now open to reveal little pockets.
• Insert garden cane/dowelling through chimney loops to hang up.
• Design of house may be adjusted to suit your area.

c Card homes

Let the children make card frontages of their own homes. Cut out the windows and cut and fold back the front door. Use scraps of materials for curtains, paper fasteners for door handles, pictures of flowers for garden areas, and so on. Add tabs to the back to stand up and write a caption on the roof suitable to your theme.

USES: *Link with a theme on thanking God for our homes and families, for food and shelter.*

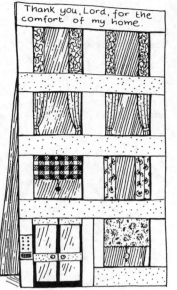

c Model pig

Cover a blown-up balloon with papier-mâché and allow to dry thoroughly. (Make sure a small hole around the knot is left unpapered.) Now pop the balloon and remove. Paste on four legs, two ears and a snout made from egg-boxes and paint the pig a pink colour. When dry, cut a slit in the top if you wish. It can be used for collecting stamps, bottle tops or your offering.

d Butterfly models

Make butterfly models as shown, with fat little plasticine bodies and decorated card wings. Push in pipe cleaners for antennae.

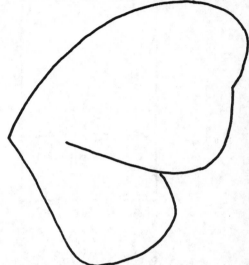

ANIMAL MODELS

a Egg-box animals

Follow the directions to make a pig or hen from egg-boxes. Small yoghurt pots can also be used.

• For pig and hen, tape two egg-box cones together.

FOR PIG
1. Paint pink.
2. Make curly tail by wrapping strip of paper tightly around pencil.

3. Cut ears.

4. Assemble using another cone cut into four for legs. Use PVA glue.

5. Draw face.

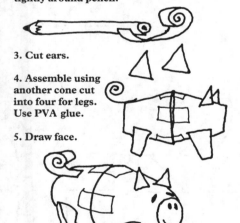

FOR HEN
1. Cover body with roughly torn pieces of brown, white or black paper.

2. Cut hen's comb, beak and feet from red paper or card.

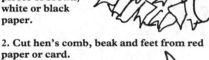

3. Assemble. Draw eyes.

• Trace this shape to make templates for butterfly wings.

• Decorate wings and push into body.

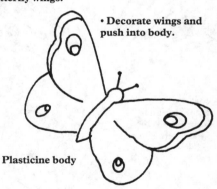

Plasticine body

b Pig faces

Make pig faces using squares of pink paper as shown.

1. Fold a square of paper across one diagonal. Open, then fold across the other diagonal.

2. Fold up a small triangle at corner A. Draw nostrils. Cut out two eyes close to the fold as shown.

3. Fold down corners B and C to form ears. Hold corner A and place in front of child's face.

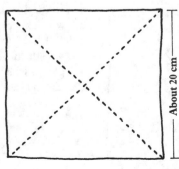

About 20 cm

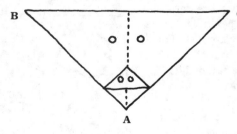

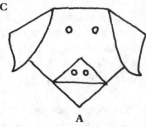

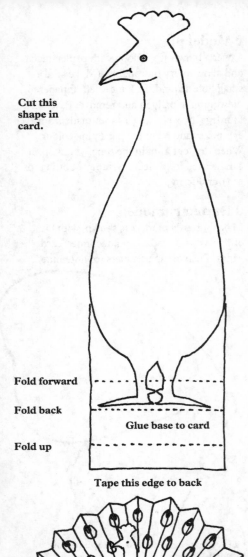

Cut this shape in card.

Fold forward

Fold back

Glue base to card

Fold up

Tape this edge to back

Make and decorate paper fan. Secure with paper-clip. Tape to back of peacock.

Completed peacock

BOATS AND FISH

a Fold-a-boat

Make paper boats as shown. Model 1 will actually sail. Model 2 will also sail but needs some ballast (eg, a lump of plasticine) to keep it on an even keel.

Model 1
Use 20 cm square of paper

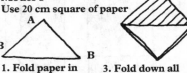

1. Fold paper in half to form triangle.

2. Fold B corners to A.

3. Fold down all thicknesses except one.

4. Turn. Fold down single layer.

5. Open this new triangle and make it flat.

6. Pulling at 'o', open out boat.

Model 2
Use 20 cm square of paper

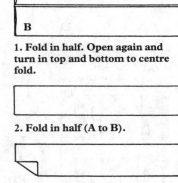

1. Fold in half. Open again and turn in top and bottom to centre fold.

2. Fold in half (A to B).

3. Turn up both corners.

4. Turn down a flap on both sides.

b Sailing boat

Make a background picture as shown and write a verse on a strip of wavy paper. Cut out a boat with two slits, then assemble the picture, the wave and the boat, stapling the wave to the picture at both ends. Now sail the boat along the sea, revealing the words of the verse.

1.

2. *Jesus said 'Courage! It is I. Don't be afraid!' Matt. 14:27.*

3.

4. *Jesus said 'Courage!' 'Don't be afraid! Matt. 14:27.'*

Staple

c Boat on wheels!

Provide a selection of small cardboard boxes for the hull, garden canes for axles, paper for sails, cotton reels or card circles for wheels and assemble as illustrated. Write a verse or caption on the sail.

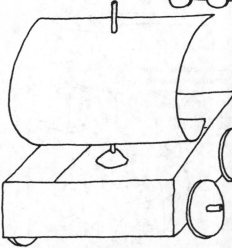

NB Use plasticine to attach the mast and sail to the base of the boat.

d Handy fish

Draw around and cut out the outline of a child's hand from stiff paper. Decorate as a fish with the fingers as the fin and tail, or as an octopus with the fingers dangling down. Tape a thin cane or straw to the back.

e Peacocks

Cut out the body of the peacock and fold as shown. Fold a piece of blue, green or grey paper concertina-style and decorate with self-adhesive spots, sequins, or circular prints made with carrots or plastic bottle tops. Fasten a paper-clip at the bottom edge of the fan and attach the tail to the back of the body with sticky tape. Mount on a base of thick card so the peacock will stand.

USES for animal models: *Link with animal themes, with a creation theme; the pigs can be linked with the parable of the lost son.*

e Peter and us

Make a display as shown, highlighting the truths Peter learnt about Jesus. The fish could be made on their own and used with other activities.

Card background

Garden canes

Sea or pond scene painted on the background

Wool or thread

Card fishes

JESUS IS WONDERFUL

JESUS

GOD ♡ ME

JESUS IS GOD'S SON

USES for boat and fish models:
Use with the Gospel stories which refer to boats, sailing, fishing, and so on.

TO MAKE FISH

• Cut slit – slot A into B   • Fold in half   • Cut slit

A   B

• For individual scenes, use A4 size card for background and plastic straw(s) instead of garden cane.

SHEEP MODELS

a Jumping sheep

Make a sheep to hang in the window, as shown.

1. Help each member of your group to cut out a cardboard sheep shape.

2. Cover the sheep in cotton wool and draw on the facial features in black felt pen.

3. Help the children to cut out a gate shape.

4. Finally, string the sheep and the gate together with thin elastic. Hang your finished sheep in the window.

b Matchbox sheep

Make an unusual sheep from empty matchboxes or other small boxes.

1. Draw sheep's face on one end.

2. Glue cotton wool all round box excluding face.

3. Thread pipe cleaners through box on both sides.

4. Bend to form legs. Use another pipe cleaner for tail.

c Stand-up sheep

Paste the sheep template on to thin card and cut it out. Fold along the dotted line, then paste the body and cover with cotton wool, and stand up.

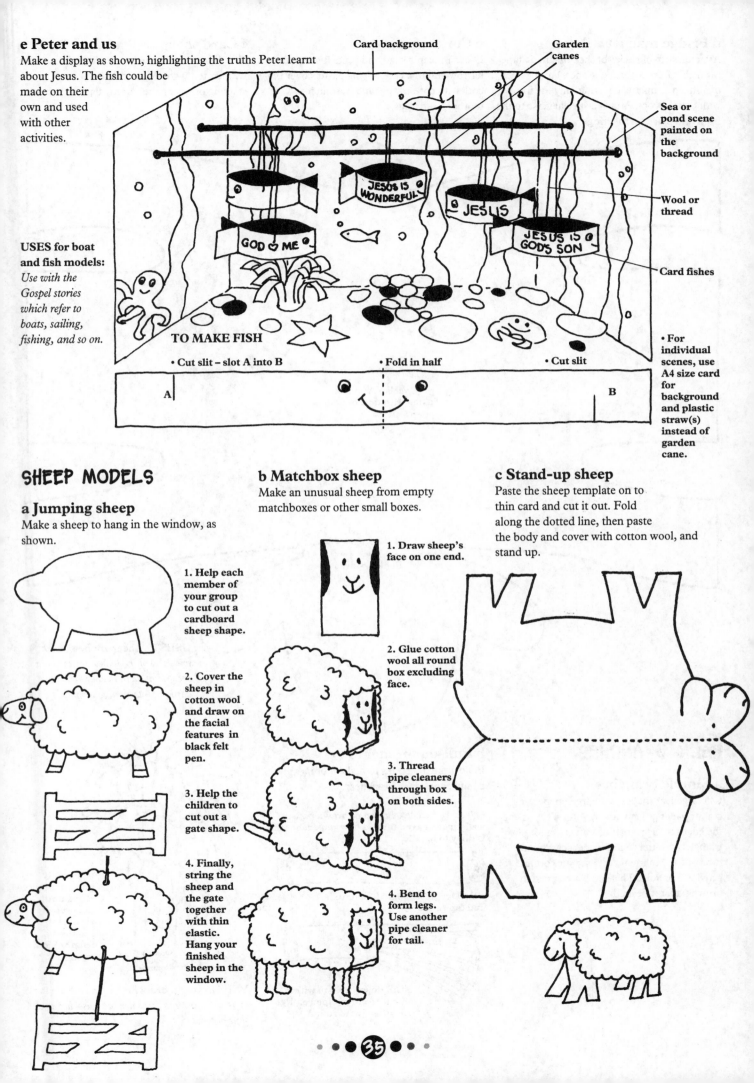

● ● ● 35 ● ● ●

d Fridge magnet

Attach a strip of sticky-backed magnetic tape (available from a good stationers) to the back of a sheep template, covering only the front with cotton wool. Attach a special verse to the front and place on the fridge.

e Cork sheep

Draw a sheep's head and paste it on to the narrow end of a cork. Using paste, cover the cork with cotton wool and push in four toothpicks for legs.

f Card sheep

Cut the outline below from card and cover with cotton wool. Make the sheep stand by stapling or taping the tummy flaps together.

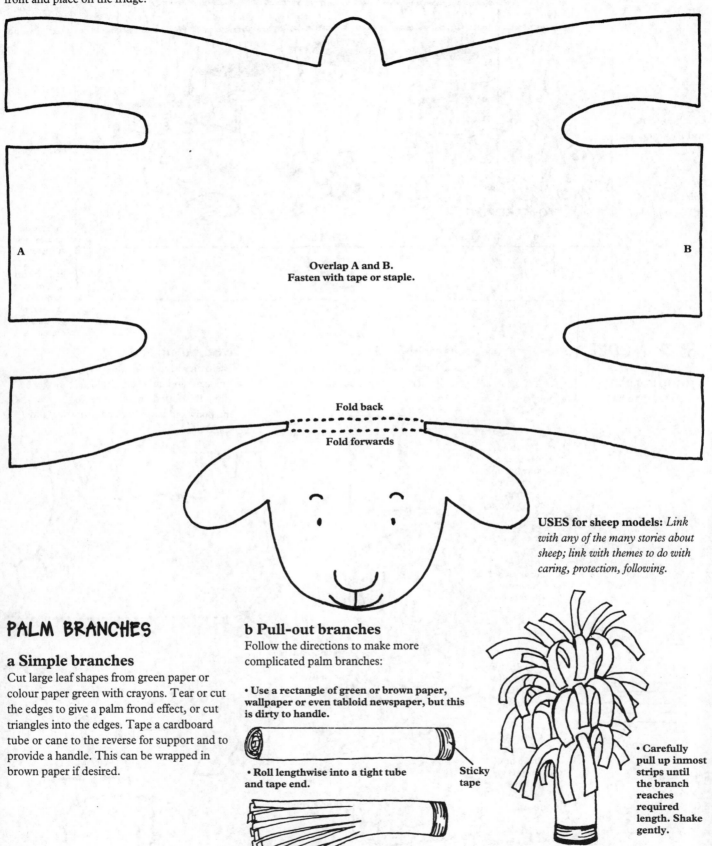

A

B

**Overlap A and B.
Fasten with tape or staple.**

Fold back

Fold forwards

USES for sheep models: Link with any of the many stories about sheep; link with themes to do with caring, protection, following.

PALM BRANCHES

a Simple branches

Cut large leaf shapes from green paper or colour paper green with crayons. Tear or cut the edges to give a palm frond effect, or cut triangles into the edges. Tape a cardboard tube or cane to the reverse for support and to provide a handle. This can be wrapped in brown paper if desired.

b Pull-out branches

Follow the directions to make more complicated palm branches:

• **Use a rectangle of green or brown paper, wallpaper or even tabloid newspaper, but this is dirty to handle.**

• **Roll lengthwise into a tight tube and tape end.**

Sticky tape

• **Cut down tube, to within about 15 cm of taped end, to make strips all round.**

• **Carefully pull up inmost strips until the branch reaches required length. Shake gently.**

USES for palm branches: *Link with the story of Jesus' entry into Jerusalem and use during a time of praise.*

MODEL TELEVISIONS

a Simple televisions

Make simple televisions as shown. Children will enjoy drawing their own pictures, pasting them on to the 'screen', and then seeing them displayed.

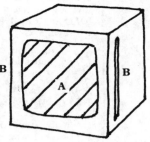

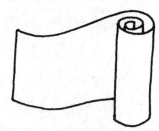

1. Choose a cardboard box any size. Cut out the shaded area A for screen. Cut slots B at each side.

2. Trim a long sheet of old wallpaper so that it will go through the slots.

3. Paste pictures on strip of paper, leaving at least 10 cm blank at each end and between each picture.

b Cereal box television

Make a more complicated television as shown, again using the children's drawings.

4. Feed paper through slots and watch.

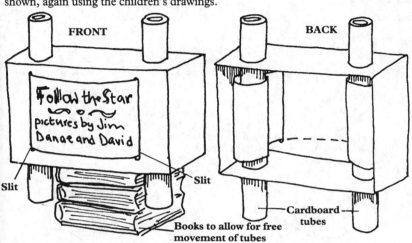

Follow the Star
pictures by Jim
Danae and David

Slit

Slit

Books to allow for free movement of tubes

FRONT

BACK

Cardboard tubes

USES for model televisions: *Use to review a story, as a visual aid, to encourage the children to think about the theme by drawing pictures about it.*

1. Remove back panel from cereal box and cut two slits in front panel as shown.

2. Cut two circles in top and bottom of long sides of box; thread through two cardboard tubes.

3. Cut a strip of paper for television screen slightly narrower than the depth of the slits.

4. Leave beginning and end 15–20 cm of paper blank to allow for feeding through and wrapping around tubes. (Tape ends to tubes.)

5. Space out pictures along strip, adding a title and 'credits' if desired.

LIGHT MODELS

a Lighthouse

Make a lighthouse as shown, carrying a message which could be changed to suit the story or theme.

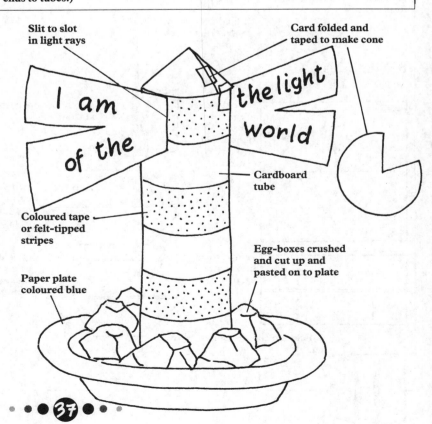

Slit to slot in light rays

Card folded and taped to make cone

I am
of the
the light
world

Cardboard tube

Coloured tape or felt-tipped stripes

Paper plate coloured blue

Egg-boxes crushed and cut up and pasted on to plate

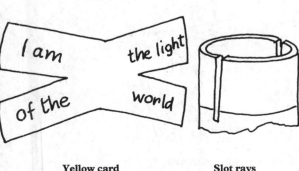

I am
of the
the light
world

Yellow card for light rays

Slot rays into top of tube

b Lantern

Make lanterns as shown, using coloured paper or by drawing a bright pattern on the paper before cutting.

USES for light models: *Link with a theme on light or on darkness; link with Jesus' teaching on being light for the world.*

1. Cut off a strip about 25 mm wide. Keep this to use as the handle.

> Jesus said, I am the light of the world. Whoever follows me will never walk in darkness, but will have the light of life.   John 8:12

2. Help the children to write the memory verse along the top of the paper.

3. Fold the paper in half horizontally, then make about 8 or 10 cuts in the paper. NB Don't cut all the way to the edge.

4. Unfold the paper and attach the ends together with sticky tape.

5. Finally, attach the handle with sticky tape and the lantern is finished.

WIND MODELS

a Balloons

Make origami balloons as shown and blow them up. Use lightweight paper.

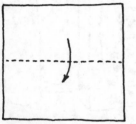

1. Fold paper (30 cm square) in half, decorating outside if wished.

2. Fold in half again.

3. Fold front corner down, to form a crease.

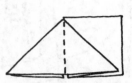

4. Fold corner out to form a triangle. Repeat 3 and 4 on reverse.

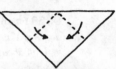

5. Fold front corners forward. Do the same on reverse.

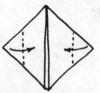

6. Fold front corners into centre. Do the same on reverse.

Hole

7. Fold front corners up and slide inside the folds. Do the same on reverse.

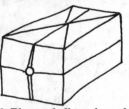

8. Blow up balloon through the hole in the top.

c Kites

Make the kites as shown, attaching long tails which can flap in the breeze.

1. Cut out required shape and size from coloured card.

2. Decorate with adhesive shapes, gummed shapes or felt-tipped pens.

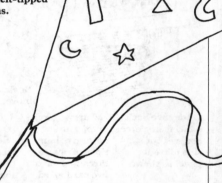

3. Add 'tail' made from gift ribbon.

4. Tape stick to the back of the kite so that it can be waved in the breeze.

USES for wind models: *Link with a theme on the wind and what it does. A link may be made with Pentecost.*

b Windmills

Make windmills as shown.

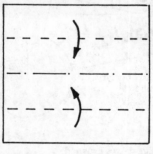

1. Fold sides of square of paper (approx. 20 cm) into centre.

2. Fold sides into centre again.

3. Fold top corner up and out.

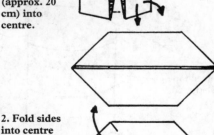

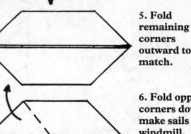

4. Fold bottom corner down and out.

5. Fold remaining two corners outward to match.

6. Fold opposite corners down to make sails of windmill.

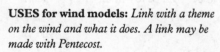

7. Attach windmill to stick with a drawing pin.

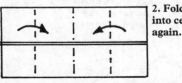

PICTURE FRAMES

a Hanging frame

Make a hanging frame as shown.

1. Cut two pieces of card 15 cm x 19.5 cm.

2. Cut a hole the size of your photo in the centre of one piece of card (piece A) to make a card frame.

3. Paste a decorated border on to the card frame. Varnish with PVA glue, slightly diluted with water.

4. Paste the decorated frame on to piece B, then paste photo to centre of frame. Add ribbon for hanging.

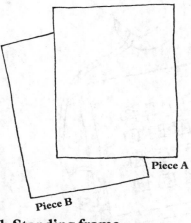

Piece B

Piece A

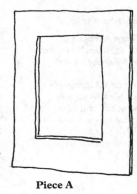

Piece A

b Standing frame

Make a standing frame as shown, enlarging the outline and using it as a template.

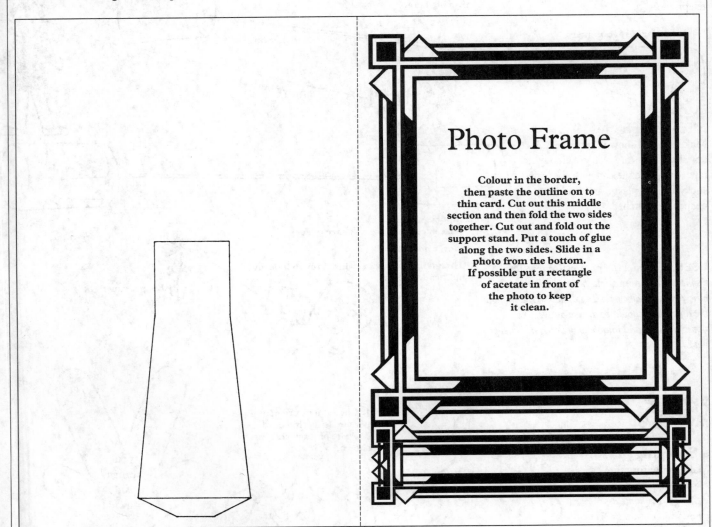

Photo Frame

Colour in the border, then paste the outline on to thin card. Cut out this middle section and then fold the two sides together. Cut out and fold out the support stand. Put a touch of glue along the two sides. Slide in a photo from the bottom. If possible put a rectangle of acetate in front of the photo to keep it clean.

c Simple frame

Cover a polystyrene meat tray with hessian or a coloured fabric and mount a picture on the front. Tape a wool loop to the back for hanging.

USES for picture frames: *Use to display photographs or special pictures the children have made; give as gifts.*

MODEL TELEPHONES

a Simple telephones

Make very simple telephones as shown, for young children to enjoy playing with.

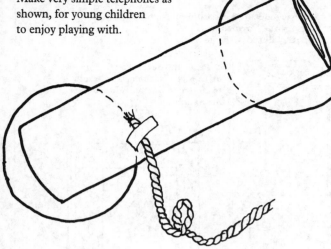

A simple handset which children can make themselves

- Glue two card circles firmly to either end of a cardboard tube.

- Tape a length of string to back of tube for telephone cord.

You could develop this idea by taping the other end of the string to a box on which you have drawn push buttons.

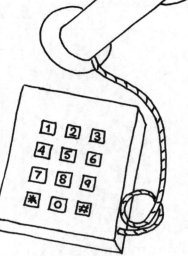

b Yoghurt pot telephone

Follow the directions to make this traditional telephone.

Yoghurt containers

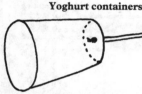

• Make hole in base. Thread string through and tie a big knot.

5–6 m string

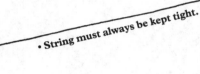

• String must always be kept tight.

c Tin can phone

Make these as shown, ensuring that any sharp parts are well-covered with tape. Decorate the can with patterned sticky-backed plastic and avoid any chance of scratches.

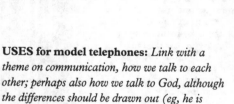

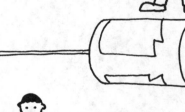

Empty cans without lids (make sure there are no sharp edges)

• Pierce hole at end.

• Thread thin string or twine through hole and knot inside cans.

Keep string tight!

USES for model telephones: *Link with a theme on communication, how we talk to each other; perhaps also how we talk to God, although the differences should be drawn out (eg, he is never engaged and unable to hear us; he is never out).*

PEOPLE MODELS

a Spinning person

Make these from thin card as shown.

USES: *Take home as a reminder of themes associated with Jesus' love.*

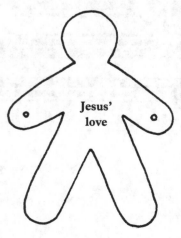

Jesus' love

1. Cut out a figure of a person using thin card.
2. Write on each side, as shown.

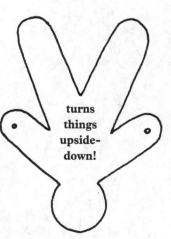

turns things upside-down!

3. Make holes in the arms and tie a piece of string through each one.
4. Spin the figure by twisting the strings between your hands.

b Nodding person

Make nodding models as shown.

USES: *Use to act out friends meeting and talking; link with stories of the early church where the Christians shared together.*

- Use card for this model.
- Also cut 2 strips – 20 cm x 2 cm.
- Pin with paper fasteners through marks.
- Make people 'talk' by pulling and pushing side tabs.

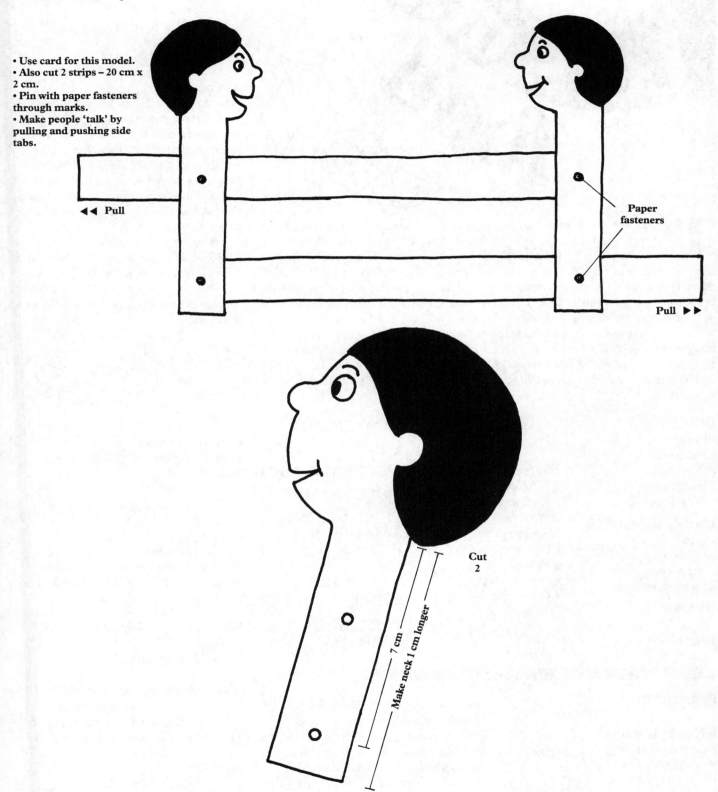

◀◀ Pull

Paper fasteners

Pull ▶▶

Cut 2

7 cm

Make neck 1 cm longer

6 Let's make food

There are very few children who don't enjoy making something and then eating it. Yet often we avoid 'cooking' activities because we don't feel we can cope with them. We worry about the mess, we don't have the time, our group is too large, our facilities aren't adequate, we haven't got a stove. Often it is possible to get around these difficulties. If time is limited or we anticipate a snowstorm with the flour, prepare most of the ingredients beforehand, letting the children help with the finishing stages. Divide into small groups of two or three to do the cooking – even at school, classes don't all cook together! Recruit some extra help for a cooking activity – a good way to involve members of your children's families you may not often see. Then there are lots of recipes and food activities that don't require special facilities or a stove; you can make sandwiches, a fruit salad, some no-cook sweets and snacks.

This section features lots of imaginative ideas for making and working with food. Why not try some!

BISCUITS
a Honey biscuits
b Easter biscuits
c Plain biscuits
d Honey balls
e Oatmeal biscuits

USING BISCUITS
a Faces
b Gingerbread people
c Star biscuits
d Party preparations

BREAD
a Bread
b Drop scones

c Chapattis
d Jewish bread

SWEETS AND SNACKS
a Marshmallow people
b Peppermint creams (younger children)
c Peppermint creams (older children)
d Coconut cakes
e Coconut ice
f Quick cakes

SANDWICHES

SOUP

PENTECOST FOOD

MOSES BASKETS

USING GRAINS AND SEEDS
a Nutty fruits
b Sesame snaps
c Cornflake cakes
d Popcorn

TALKABOUT COOKING

BISCUITS

a Honey biscuits

Preheat oven: 180°C, 350°F, gas mark 4
You will need:
225g (8oz) self-raising flour
110g (4oz) butter or margarine
110g (4oz) soft brown sugar
1 egg
1 rounded tablespoon of honey
Few drops of vanilla essence
Flaked almonds to decorate

What to do: Cream the butter and sugar until soft. Add the egg and vanilla essence, then beat in the honey. Sift the flour and add it to the mixture to make a firm dough. Spoon out rounded teaspoons of the mixture and roll into balls. Place about six or eight on a greased baking tray. Slightly flatten each biscuit with your fingers and decorate with a piece of flaked almond. Bake in the centre of the oven for 15 minutes or until golden brown.

Makes about 30 biscuits.

USES: *The Bible tells us that manna tasted a little like biscuits made with honey (Exodus 16:31), so these biscuits link with the Israelites' story.*

b Easter biscuits

Preheat oven: 180°C, 350°F, gas mark 4
You will need:
340g (12oz) self-raising flour
1 tsp mixed spice
1 tsp cinnamon
175g (6oz) margarine
175g (6oz) sugar
110g (4oz) currants
2 beaten eggs
Icing sugar

What to do: Put the first four ingredients in a bowl, and rub in the margarine until the mixture resembles breadcrumbs. Stir in the sugar and currants, add the beaten eggs and knead to a dough. Roll out to a thickness of 0.5cm on a floured board, then cut into rounds with a fluted cutter. Place on a baking sheet and bake for 15-20 minutes until golden brown. Cool before icing.

Makes about 12 biscuits.

USES: *Make the biscuits with the children, or, if not possible, let the children simply ice crosses on the biscuits for decoration. Use this traditional biscuit to link with the Easter story; icing crosses add to the link.*

c Plain biscuits

Preheat oven: 180°C, 350°F, gas mark 4
You will need:
225g (8oz) plain flour
110g (4oz) caster sugar
110g (4oz) margarine
1 egg
Juice of 1 lemon

What to do: Mix flour and sugar and rub in margarine. Add egg and lemon juice and mix to a dough. Roll out thinly and cut into rounds. Bake for 15 minutes.

For decorating you will need:
Saucers
Round-ended knives
Icing sugar
Decorations: small sweets, jelly sweets, *Smarties*, 'hundreds and thousands'

Let the children help decorate these biscuits. Make the icing up together, then put a little

on a saucer for two or three children to use. Place small amounts of decorations in little pots for the children to share.

USES: *Link with a sharing/caring theme; give to members of the church family who are unwell, unable to get out or missing from your group.*

d Honey balls

This simple recipe requires no cooking and children will enjoy the texture of the mixture as they knead it and roll it into balls.

Choose a cup as a measure.

Place into a large bowl:

¹/₂ cup honey (or corn syrup)

¹/₂ cup peanut butter

1 cup dried milk

1 cup rolled oats

Mix all ingredients together well, then divide into about 24 pieces. Knead lightly by hand and shape into balls. Each ball could be rolled  in coconut, 'hundreds and thousands' or chocolate or sugar strands.

Makes 24 honey balls.

e Oatmeal biscuits

Preheat oven: 160°C, 325°F, gas mark 3

You will need:

225g (8oz) margarine

275g (10oz) soft brown sugar

200g (7oz) rolled oats

5 tblspns milk

275g (10oz) self-raising flour

What to do:

Cream the margarine and sugar. Stir in the oats, milk and flour to form a soft dough. Chill in the refrigerator.

With the children: Divide the dough into small portions. Roll out to about 0.5cm thickness then cut with biscuit cutters. Bake on greased baking trays for 10–15 minutes.

This recipe can be prepared beforehand leaving the children to roll out and cut out the biscuits.

USES: *Use to give the children the experience of preparing food as Martha did, and for the fun of sharing work with friends.*

USING BISCUITS

a Faces

You will need:

Yellow icing

Plain biscuits

2 blue *Smarties*

6 brown *Smarties*

Utensils:

Plastic knife

Bowl (to hold icing)

Tray (to work on)

Provide ingredients and utensils for making faces. Make the four illustrated cards (as shown) to help younger children follow the instructions.

USES: *Link with a 'following instructions' theme, a preparing theme, and with parties.*

b Gingerbread people

Make up biscuit dough for the children to roll out and shape into people (perhaps using cutters), or into faces, then choose from a variety of ingredients to decorate (cherries, peel, currants).

USES: *Link with the theme that we are all different just as each biscuit person is different, but we are all special to the person who made us.*

c Star biscuits

Provide plain biscuits, water icing and small stencil cut-outs of stars. Paste the icing over the stencil on to the biscuit. Lift the stencil off very carefully.

USES: *Link with a Christmas theme.*

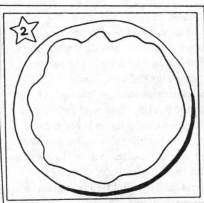

1. When making this card, colour in the biscuit, yellow icing and brown and blue *Smarties*.

2. Colour the biscuit and icing.

3. Draw as for card 2 but add blue *Smarties*.

4. Draw as for card 3 but add brown *Smarties*.

d Party preparations

Use plain biscuits or cakes and ice them using blunt knives or the backs of spoons. Decorate with silver balls, vermicelli, glacé cherries, 'hundreds and thousands', sugar strands, and so on.

USES: *Talk about preparing for parties and making sure there is enough for everyone.*

BREAD

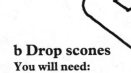

a Bread

Provide children with some experience of making bread. This could be mixing the yeast, flour and water to form a dough, kneading and shaping loaves, baking ready-shaped dough or simply observing how the dough rises – and, of course, eating and enjoying the warm bread at the end.

Oven temperature: 220°C, 425°F, gas mark 7 (not essential to preheat, see below)

You will need:

500g (18oz) strong bread flour
2 tsps salt
5g (1/4oz) vegetable fat
1 packet dried yeast
250ml (9 fluid oz) warm water

What to do: Sieve the flour and salt into a bowl. Rub in the vegetable fat and add the dried yeast (following manufacturer's instructions). Make a hollow in the centre of the mixture and pour in the warm water. Mix carefully and thoroughly. Turn out on to a lightly floured surface.

Flour hands, then knead dough for about 10 minutes. Replace in bowl, cover and leave to rise for at least 30 minutes. Then divide the dough among the children (about 12–15 children for this quantity). Flour hands before touching the dough, then knead and shape for baking. Place rolls/shapes on a well-greased baking tray and, while the oven heats to the required temperature, leave to rise in a warm place. Brush with beaten egg or milk just before baking. Bake for 20–25 minutes. Allow to cool before eating!

Makes 12–15 rolls.

b Drop scones

You will need:

110g (4 oz) self-raising flour
Pinch of salt
25g (1oz) sugar
1 egg
150ml (1/4 pint) milk
25g (1oz) melted margarine

With children: Sift flour and salt into a bowl, then add sugar. Add egg and milk and beat to a smooth batter. Stir in the margarine.

Adults only: Grease and warm a griddle or heavy-based pan. Drop tablespoonfuls of the mixture on to the hot griddle, allowing space for spreading. Cook for about 2 minutes. When scones are slightly puffed up and covered with bubbles, turn and brown other sides. Keep the first batch moist by wrapping in a clean tea towel while the rest are cooking.

Makes about 14 drop scones.

c Chapattis

Prepare the dough ahead of time and have the children roll out the portions ready for frying. Chapattis are cooked quickly.

You will need:

500g (18oz) wholewheat flour
1/2 tsp salt
2 tblspns melted margarine
200ml (7 fluid oz) water

What to do: Combine flour and salt in a bowl, then stir in margarine and add about three-quarters of the water, sprinkling on an additional 1 or 2 tablespoons of the water, if needed, to make a soft dough that can be kneaded. Knead well, then cover the mixture with a damp cloth and leave to rest for an hour. Then divide into as many portions as you need, rolling out each one to about 0.5cm thick. Cook each chapatti in a heavy, greased frying pan for about 2 minutes on each side. Eat at once or keep in a warm oven until ready to serve.

USES: *Make these as an example of unleavened bread.*

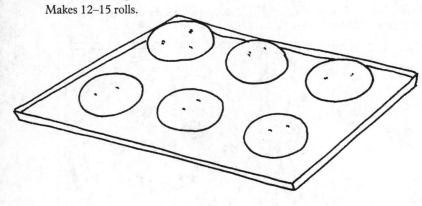

c Peppermint creams (older children)

You will need:

   250g (9oz) icing sugar
   $1\frac{1}{2}$ tblspns milk
   Peppermint essence
   Green food colouring (optional)
   Paper sweet cases

What to do: Sift icing sugar into a bowl, add milk, a few drops of peppermint essence and one drop of green food colouring if desired. Mix with a wooden spoon until the mixture is bound together and has the texture of plasticine. If the mixture becomes too wet, add a little extra icing sugar. If the mixture is too stiff, add one or two drops of milk. Shape into small balls about the size of marbles. Roll each ball in granulated sugar and place in a paper sweet case.

A simple presentation box can be made out of a small square of cardboard. Cut along the bold lines and fold along the dotted lines (as shown). Fix the sides in place with a stapler.

Makes about 22–24 sweets.

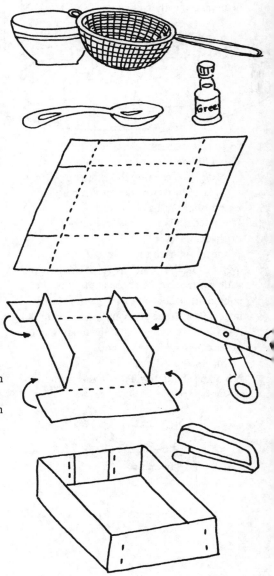

d Jewish bread

Preheat oven: 230°C, 450°F, gas mark 8

You will need:

   50g (2oz) butter or margarine
   500g (18oz) strong plain flour
   20g (small 1oz) caster sugar
   1 medium egg
   25g (1oz) fresh yeast
   185ml (6 fluid oz) tepid water
   5g ($\frac{1}{4}$oz) salt
   Sesame or poppy seeds to decorate

What to do: Sieve flour into basin, rub in butter or margarine. Mix sugar, salt and egg together. Mix yeast with water and leave for a few minutes to become frothy. Add all other ingredients to the flour mixture to form a rough dough. Turn out on to a floured working surface and knead and flatten for about 10 minutes (children enjoy this!). Then let dough rest for 10 minutes. Now divide dough into strands and twist or plait together. Place on a greased baking sheet, cover with a cloth, then leave for 45 minutes in a warm place until rolls have doubled in size. When ready to bake, brush with milk, then decorate with the seeds. Bake for 20-25 minutes.

   Makes 14 rolls.

SWEETS AND SNACKS

a Marshmallow people

Make a special 'person sweet' for family members.

You will need:

   Marshmallows
   Melted chocolate
   Cocktail sticks
   Baking cases

What to do: Spear the marshmallows with the cocktail sticks and dip the end into the melted chocolate (for hair). Then dip a second stick into the chocolate and use like a pencil to draw a face. Lay in the baking case and when the chocolate has hardened, remove the stick.

b Peppermint creams (younger children)

You will need:

   White of 1 egg (you may prefer to use *dried* egg white here)
   300g (11oz) icing sugar
   Peppermint essence

What to do: Whisk egg white until frothy. Gradually beat in 200g (7oz) icing sugar and add a few drops of peppermint essence. Turn mixture on to board and knead in remaining sugar. Roll into long sausage. Cut into 0.5cm slices, then shape into rounds. Leave to dry.

   Makes 25-30 sweets.

d Coconut cakes

You will need:

    250g (9oz) icing sugar
    200ml (6 fluid oz) condensed milk
    250g (9oz) desiccated coconut
    Food colouring
    Sweets (for decoration)
    Small baking cases

What to do: Mix together icing sugar, condensed milk, desiccated coconut and a few drops of food colouring in a large bowl. Mix well until thickened. Form into shapes adding a sweet to the top of each one and place in baking cases.

e Coconut ice

You will need:

    150 g (5oz) desiccated coconut
    300g (11oz) icing sugar
    4–5 tblspns evaporated milk

What to do: Combine coconut and icing sugar, then add milk and mix to a stiff consistency. Turn out and knead until smooth. Shape into bars and leave to dry on a plate dusted with icing sugar.

f Quick cakes

You will need:

    110g (4oz) cooking chocolate
    3 teacupfuls cornflakes or rice crispies
    2 tblspns raisins or sultanas
    Grated rind of a lemon or orange
    Baking cases

What to do: Melt the chocolate in a bowl over a pan of hot water (requires adult help or adult supervision). Chocolate may then be poured into a cooler bowl to prevent burnt fingers. Mix in the cornflakes, raisins and rind. Spoon tablespoons of the mixture into paper cases and leave to cool.

Makes about 12 cakes.

NB Some children will prefer this without the raisins and rind.

SANDWICHES

Provide slices of ready-cut bread and let children butter them and then choose a spread to put on them from such things as peanut butter, jam, cheese spread, and so on. Eat in the session or cut and wrap each sandwich to eat later.

USES: *Talk about the different types of fillings and where they come from; link with the feeding of the five thousand (sandwiches are a common lunch today); link with a bread theme.*

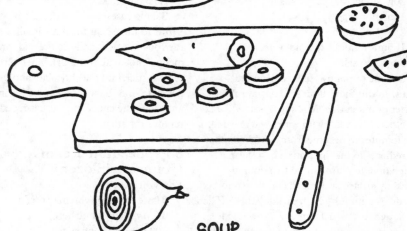

SOUP

Give children the experience of preparing food by helping them to make soup. Wash hands, then provide chopping boards and fairly blunt knives. The vegetables they prepare will therefore need to be soft, eg, peeled tomatoes or harder vegetables already cut into thin strips. Add herbs, seasoning and water or stock. When cooked, pour into small containers for the children to smell, taste and enjoy.

USES: *Use as an opportunity to talk about the variety and abundance of food God gives to us.*

PENTECOST FOOD

Prepare some Pentecost food to link with the festival.

- **Bread:** children arrange part-baked rolls or loaves on baking trays and an adult places them in the oven. If preferred, use the Jewish Bread recipe.
- **Fruit salad:** have the children prepare fresh fruit; for younger children, choose fruit which can be cut with blunt knives or prepared by hand.
- **Cheesecake:** mix up a packet cheesecake together, having prepared the base beforehand.

USES: *Link with Pentecost, talking about preparing food for special days and about the enjoyment of cooking and eating special food.*

USING GRAINS AND SEEDS

a Nutty fruits
You will need:
>   200g (7oz) assorted dried fruits
>   10ml (1 tblspn) thick honey
>   Desiccated coconut

What to do: Chop all the fruit to sultana size. Mix with honey until the fruit is covered. Divide mixture into 10-12 pieces, shape into balls and roll each in coconut until well coated.

>   Makes about 12 fruits.

b Sesame snaps
Preheat oven: 180°C, 350°F, gas mark 4
You will need:
>   200g (7oz) medium oatmeal
>   75g (3oz) roasted sesame seeds
>   6 tblspns honey
>   6 tblspns oil (sesame oil if possible)
>   75g (3oz) muscovado sugar

What to do: Combine all ingredients in a bowl and mix well. Tip mixture on to a Swiss roll tin and smooth out. Cook for 20-25 minutes. Cut into squares while still warm, then leave to cool.

>   Makes about 16-20.

c Cornflake cakes
You will need:
>   110g (4oz) cooking chocolate
>   150g (5oz) cornflakes
>   Baking cases

What to do: Melt the chocolate in a bowl over hot water or in a microwave oven. Remove chocolate from heat and stir in cornflakes until all are covered with chocolate. Spoon into cake cases and leave to cool.
Makes about 12.

MOSES BASKETS

You will need:
>   110g (4oz) cooking chocolate
>   3 shredded wheats, crumbled
>   Baking cases
>   Fondant icing/marzipan to mould 'Baby Moses' figures

>   Makes about 10–12 baskets.

If time is limited, complete the baskets by just doing stage 4.

USES: *Link with the story of God's care for baby Moses and his choice of Moses to help his people.*

1. Melt chocolate in a bowl (do not overheat).

2. Add crushed shredded wheat until the correct consistency is reached. Obviously, the more baskets needed the greater the quantities required.

3. Place the mixture in paper cases and press with the bowl of a spoon until the mixture becomes 'basket' shaped. Leave to cool.

4. Provide the children with fondant icing or other edible material and let them mould some 'Baby Moses' shapes to place into the baskets.

d Popcorn

You will need:

    25g (1oz) margarine

    50g (2oz) popping corn

What to do: Melt margarine in a strong, large saucepan with a lid. Add the corn. Place lid on firmly and shake frequently over a medium heat. Listen to the popping and pinging, still shaking gently. When all popping has ceased, remove from heat and tip into a large bowl. Eat while still warm. Add melted butter and a sprinkle of salt for salty popcorn. Toss in a little melted runny honey for sweet popcorn.

    Makes a large bowlful.

TALKABOUT COOKING

Scrambled eggs are simple to make and interesting to talk about. At each stage, look carefully at the egg and have the children describe what it looks like (egg in shell, cracked egg, whisked egg, cooking egg). Other ideas for talking about are: make a jelly, stir a milky dessert, make a fruit squash or a milk shake, prepare a fruit salad.

7 Let's make clay

Have you ever enjoyed the fun of sinking your hands into a pool of cool, wet mud, squeezing hard and watching the mud ooze out in little trickles between your fingers? Delightful! Touch is a very important God-given sense, and the activity of modelling allows children to experience and experiment with texture, with pressing, rolling, pulling and squeezing a malleable substance.

The playdough and clay suggested in this section are somewhat cleaner and easier to manage than mud, and children will enjoy the opportunity of making pots or prints, or of simply exploring the qualities of the material. Cooked playdough will last several weeks if stored in an airtight container in the fridge. Items made from baking clay, if properly baked, will keep for years. Don't leave this activity for the children to do on their own – enjoy it with them!

In the following pages you will find:

PLAYDOUGH RECIPES
a 'No-cook' playdough
b 'Cooked' playdough
c Baking clay

WATER JARS
OIL LAMPS
THUMB POTS

PASTA ORNAMENTS
BADGES AND PENDANTS
HANDPRINTS

PLAYDOUGH RECIPES

a 'No-cook' playdough
This recipe involves no cooking and is therefore simple to use with children although it will not last quite as long as the cooked variety.

For every 4–6 children, you will need:
  2 cups plain flour
  1 cup salt
  1 cup water
  A few drops food colouring
  1 tblspn of cooking oil

What to do: Mix the flour and salt together. Little by little add the liquid (including the food colouring and the cooking oil) to the flour and salt, stirring well. When all the ingredients are combined, knead the dough on a floured surface.

b 'Cooked' playdough
Prepare this dough ahead of time as it needs time to cool, although children will enjoy its 'just warm' feel and texture.

You will need:
  1 cup flour
  1/2 cup salt
  1 tblspn oil
  1 cup water (add drops of food colouring)
  2 tsps cream of tartar

What to do: Mix all the ingredients together in a large saucepan to form a smooth paste. Cook slowly over a gentle heat until the dough leaves the sides of the pan to form a ball. Turn out, cool and knead.

Makes enough for 4.

c Baking clay
Preheat oven: 150°C, 300°F, gas mark 2
You will need:
  4 cups of flour
  1 cup of salt
  1 cup of hot water

What to do: Mix the hot water and salt. Add the flour and mix to produce a soft but not sticky or crumbly dough. This can then be modelled as desired or cut out with pastry cutters. Glaze with milk or paint the items. Bake for about two hours.

Makes enough for 4–6 children.

WATER JARS
Make little water jars from plasticine, playdough or new clay (this dries naturally without firing):
1 Roll a piece of the chosen material into a ball.
2 Hold the ball in one hand and press your other thumb into the ball.
3 Wriggle it around to make a fairly big hole.
4 Pull up sides gently until it is the size you want.
5 Smooth the sides inside and out.
6 Flatten the base so the pot will stand.
7 Attach small handles at the side if required.
USES: *Link with life in Bible times, how water was collected, carried and stored; also with the stone water jars in the wedding at Cana.*

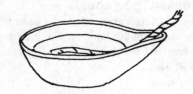

OIL LAMPS

Use new clay, playdough or plasticine to make oil lamps. Make as for water jars, but pinch to make a 'spout' to hold the wick, and add a handle if desired. Include a small piece of string for a wick. Clay lamps can be painted with terracotta-coloured poster paint once they have hardened – in this case, add the wick after painting.

USES: *Link with life in Bible times, explaining that lamps such as these were used before electricity; also with the parable of the ten girls and their oil lamps.*

THUMB POTS

Make small thumb pots or coil pots from new clay or baking clay. Encourage the children to try again if they are not satisfied with their first attempt. Paint and varnish the pots when dry.

USES: *Link with life in Bible times; also with Jeremiah in the potter's house.*

PASTA ORNAMENTS

Provide playdough in a variety of colours. Roll out small amounts to a 5mm thickness, then push pasta shapes into the dough. These will dry hard in a few days. For added effect, spray the pasta shapes beforehand with gold or silver paint.

BADGES AND PENDANTS

Use the baking clay recipe to make badges and pendants on a particular theme. For a badge open a safety-pin and push it into the clay, leaving the pin sticking outwards before baking, or glue one on to the back of the badge after baking. For a pendant, push a paper-clip halfway into the top of a shape before baking. Glaze with milk, or paint before baking, or varnish afterwards.

USES: *Use to illustrate a particular theme, eg, the dove model to link with the Holy Spirit. Badges can be taken home as reminders.*

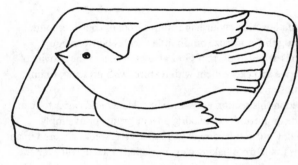

HANDPRINTS

Roll out portions of playdough and encourage the children to press their hands (and fingers, elbows, etc.) into the flattened pieces. They will see the print of their skin, and this will promote an interest in the marks, bumps and ridges that make up their skin pattern.

Alternatively, place a portion of baking clay on a paper plate as a mould and have the children press their hand in it to make a hand print. These can then be baked and taken home to give as a gift.

USES: *Examining skin patterns encourages the children to marvel at God's creation; link with themes on 'my body', 'creation', God using my hands, and so on.*

8 Let's make badges

SHAPED CARD BADGES

a General badges

Prepare templates for shaped badges to link with a story or theme, eg, lightning, star or foot shapes.

Cut out
foot shape in card.
Write on it and colour in.
Tape safety-pin to
back.

Badges are a great favourite with children, both for collecting and for making. I have seen badges in a teenager's collection made when he was a child of play-group age. Badges can be used to highlight a theme, to give as a gift, to build a group identity, to serve as a reminder of a teaching point. They are simple to make, often requiring nothing more than a card shape, a safety-pin and some imagination. Clay badges are also very effective, and a recipe and illustration for these can be found in 'Let's make clay' (page 49).

Experiment with some of the following:

CIRCLE BADGES
a General badges
b 'Sunday' circle badge
c 'God is special' badges

SHAPED CARD BADGES
a General badges
b Gift badges

READY-MADE BADGES

SHEEP BADGE

DOVE BADGE

CIRCLE BADGES

a General badges

Cut out a circle of card for each badge (or provide blank ready-made badges). Always have plenty ready as children are likely to make mistakes and want to start afresh. You will need a safety-pin and sticky tape for each badge. The badges can be designed in any number of ways (see illustration): by drawing, writing, colouring in letters or symbols, pasting on pictures from magazines or old greetings cards.

b 'Sunday' circle badge

On a yellow card circle write, 'Sunday is a special day', and let the children write their names on the back and draw rays around the edge of the sun which could be cut out. Attach a safety-pin to the back with sticky tape.

USES: *Use to talk about why Sunday is a special day for members of God's family, linking to the creation story or to Easter.*

c 'God is special' badges

On card circles write, 'I (then heart shape) God' or 'God is number 1' or 'It's great to be a friend of God'. Decorate and attach a safety-pin to the back.

USES: *Link with the theme of friendship; use as a reminder that God wants to be our special friend.*

b Gift badges

Have available a variety of card shapes (star, flower, teddy, etc.) so children can choose one for each member of their family and decorate them to make personalised badges, adding an appropriate message.

Another option is to put the names of group members in a hat and have each child pick one, then ask the person they have picked to choose their favourite badge shape, colours, and picture or theme.

Each child can then decorate the badge just as the person would like it. Add a safety-pin to the back and give it as a gift.

READY-MADE BADGES

Prepare badge designs, then photocopy them and give to the children to colour in, paste on to card and finish off with a safety-pin behind.

USES: *Use if emphasising a particular theme or to build up a group identity.*

Colour in, paste on to card, cut out and tape safety-pin to back.

SHEEP BADGE

Cut out a card sheep from a photocopied and reduced template ('Let's make templates', pages 89–91). Colour in the legs and head black, then wind white wool around the body section, making it soft and fat. When completed, attach a safety-pin to the back.

USES: *Use to accompany a sheep theme; wear as a reminder that we are like sheep and that 'The Lord is our shepherd'.*

DOVE BADGE

Use the template on page 90 ('Let's make templates') to make dove badges from white card. Colour the eye and beak and attach a safety-pin to the back.

USES: *Link with the stories of Jesus' baptism, the coming of the Holy Spirit, or with a peace theme.*

9 Let's make friezes, collages and posters

• FRIEZES

ANGEL FRIEZE
Prepare different sizes of angel cut-outs (see 'Let's make templates', page 94) from white paper. Colour with paint or crayon, or decorate with collage materials such as strips of silver foil (eg, from sweet wrappers), paper doilies or little strips of coloured tissue. Paste the completed figures on to a dark background (paint dark blue or use black or dark blue paper). Add stars and glitter.
USES: *Link with a Christmas theme of praise for the birth of Jesus.*

SHEEP FRIEZE
Use the templates from 'Let's make templates' on pages 89–91, to make paper cut-outs of sheep which can be collaged using cotton wool for the fleeces, lollipop sticks for the legs and buttons for the eyes (colour in the eyes for very young children). Each child could make one sheep. Enlarge and cut out the shepherd figure striding out ahead of the sheep, using brightly-coloured material scraps for his clothes. Make sure he is smiling. Mount the shepherd on a wall and paste the sheep on a background of wallpaper at different levels to make them appear to be skipping along behind him. The frieze could go right around the room. Write the child's name under their picture.
USES: *Link with a sheep story or theme, and use the activity to talk about how Jesus knows each child's name, just as the shepherd knows the names of his sheep.*

This section has been divided into three parts, the divisions based loosely on the following characteristics:

Friezes are scenes or pictures designed to be presented on strips of paper and attached to a wall. It is possible (but costly) to buy rolls of coloured frieze paper which can greatly enhance a scene. A cheap and very adequate alternative is to use the reverse side of wallpaper strips or, even better, to use rolls of decorator's lining paper, which can be painted or pasted on as required.

Collages are made from scraps of readily available odds and ends of materials, ranging from paper to wood shavings, from feathers to pasta shapes. As used here, they are combined in a variety of ways and pasted on to a background to present a theme-related design or picture. Collage-making is valuable in its own right in encouraging children to explore a variety of materials, to experiment with creating their own pictures, and, for younger children, to learn to use scissors.

The posters suggested are not dissimilar to the collages, but tend only to use paper or paint rather than a wider range of materials. They also tend to depend on words to a greater degree in communicating a message.

Paste is an essential element. A PVA adhesive (school glue) is best to use, although glue sticks are sometimes easier for smaller tasks (but expensive!). Store the paste in air-tight containers – plastic film containers are ideal, can be easily refilled and children tend not to use as much paste. Glue firmly on to round plastic lids so they are less likely to fall over – the lid can provide a tray for spreaders. Buy spreaders or make your own by cutting up the plastic lids of ice cream containers. Pasting the background sheet rather than individual small items (like shells) is an important tip for children to learn and cuts down on the mess. But don't forget to have aprons, soapy water and towels, small plastic containers and lots of newspaper and/or polythene sheeting available. Enjoy creating!

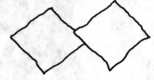

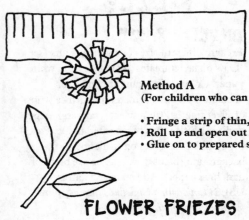

Method A
(For children who can use scissors)

• Fringe a strip of thin, coloured paper.
• Roll up and open out fringes.
• Glue on to prepared stalks.

Method B
(No cutting required)

• Tear thin, coloured paper into small pieces.
• Crush tightly or loosely.
• Glue into position.

FLOWER FRIEZES

a Making flowers

Use one of the above methods (A or B) for making flower heads, then paste on to a frieze as described. Use tissue paper, crêpe paper, coloured toilet tissue, or pieces of coloured paper, eg, cut from magazines.

b Radiant flower frieze

Prepare a large sheet of frieze paper with a blue background and bold strokes of green marker for the stems and leaves. Use bright tissue paper for the flowers and attach with paste or double-sided sticky tape.
USES: *Link with a colour theme, an Easter theme, a theme to do with growing things, a season's theme. A visually impaired child could take part using the crushed paper method of flower-making.*

c Garden frieze

Draw stalks and leaves on a background sheet, then place flower heads on to ready-pasted areas. Paint cardboard egg-boxes different shades of brown, and when dry, crush and paste along the bottom for soil. Clouds and sun could be added using cotton wool or screwed up pieces of tissue paper.
USES: *Use with a water/rain theme – flowers can't grow without water, or use as above.*

BREAD FRIEZE

Make a wall frieze to show the different stages of bread-making. The frieze could be very simple or it could be quite detailed, depending on the time and resources available (see below). Six stages might be a good number to aim for. Just as bread involves many people working together, from the seed-planting stage to the stage at which it is ready for eating, so make this a group activity, helping the children to work together as a team.

USES: *Link with a bread or food theme, with a harvest theme, or with a theme of God as provider. Make it informative for children who may have been unaware of the connection between wheat in the field and bread on the table. Link with making bread (see 'Let's make food', page 44–45).*

PEOPLE FRIEZES

a Happy crowd frieze

Provide pieces of paper on which children can draw a happy person. Cut around these roughly then paste together on a large sheet to form a happy crowd.
USES: *Use with stories which feature crowds, eg, stories about Jesus, Acts 2, stories from the Exodus. Link with the children's own experiences of crowds, the events they were attending and their feelings at the noise and bustle.*

BREAD FRIEZE

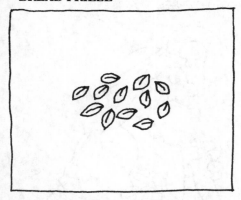

1. Tiny seeds are planted in the ground.

2. God sends the rain and sun so the seeds grow.

3. The fully grown wheat is cut and collected.

4. The wheat is crushed into flour.

5. The flour is mixed with water, salt, fat and yeast to make dough.

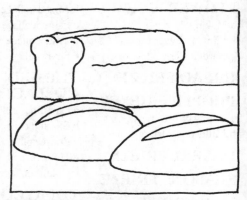

6. The dough is cooked to make bread.

b Multi-racial frieze

Prepare a pale blue background, tear green paper and paste on for grass. Produce previously cut-out pictures of children from other lands (use magazines, advertisements, or use templates to make people which the children can then colour in appropriately). Paste these on to the frieze.

USES: *Use when talking about different nationalities; link with a theme of friendship between different races, with a welcoming theme, or with an 'everyone is special to God' theme.*

DESERT FRIEZE

On a background sheet, paste torn pieces of yellow, orange or beige paper to represent the sand and rocks of a desert. Paint a blue sky or paste on strips of blue paper for the sky. Add a river if required.

USES: *Use in Bible stories which feature a desert scene, eg, the temptations of Jesus, John the Baptist preaching in the desert, God's call to Moses, Abraham's journeys.*

SEASONS FRIEZE

Make a frieze appropriate to the season, either one frieze per season, or feature four seasons on one frieze. Select materials according to the season in your country, eg, tissue paper for flowers, fine sawdust for snow, fabric of an appropriate colour for trees, bushes, sun and clouds, fallen leaves of various colours, coloured paper cut from magazines or catalogue pages for other leaves and green grass.

USES: *Link with a creation theme, with God's provision and care for his world, eg, Psalm 104.*

FISH FRIEZE

Draw, paint, print, crayon and cut out all sorts of fish shapes – the stranger the better. Mount on strips of blue frieze paper and cover with cellophane or clear plastic to give a watery illusion.

USES: *Substitute groups of animals or birds for the fish, changing the background as appropriate. Link with an animal theme, a creation theme, or a theme to do with God's provision, as above.*

● COLLAGES

BASIC COLLAGE STYLES

a Touch collage

Make an abstract design by fixing differently textured materials to a background of firm cardboard (eg, a section of a cardboard carton). Try different fabrics, sandpaper, smooth plastic, feathers, cotton wool, and so on.

b Mixed collage

Cut up pieces of coloured card or paper and provide paste and brushes. In separate dishes, place a variety of attractive materials for pasting on to the card, eg, shiny paper, fabric scraps, lace or ribbon remnants, milk bottle tops, crayon shavings, cut-up paper doilies, coloured paper, dried flower petals, sawdust, wood shavings. Once you start looking, you will find many more suitable items.

c Fabric collage

Make a large wall collage as a group project, or smaller, individual ones which can be mounted together. Provide pieces of 'rich-looking' fabric – brocade, shiny lining materials, velvet, velveteen – in lush colours

such as emerald, purple, deep red. Cut into small pieces for ease of handling.

d Pasta collage

Provide stiff card or cardboard, paste and a variety of different types of pasta. Cover the card with small areas of paste and lay on the pasta to make a pattern. When dry, spray with gold or silver paint.

e Shiny collage

Have ready a large sheet of paper and plenty of scraps of orange, yellow, silver and gold paper (try shiny sweet wrappers and the reverse of metallic gift wrap). In the centre of the paper write words of joy and celebration such as 'Jesus is the Son of God', cutting the letters from brightly-coloured paper or colouring them in. Cut the shiny paper into triangles and slashes and paste them around the words so that they appear to be coming out from the centre. Finish by pasting areas and sprinkling with glitter or use glitter glue.

USES for collages: *Link with themes on the senses, focusing on touch, sight and perhaps sound, as the collages are assembled. Link also with stories of Jesus healing blind people – a visually impaired child would be able to enjoy some of these activities. Links could also be made with the wide variety to be found in God's world, with celebration themes, with exploring patterns (thinking also of patterns in nature), with the abilities God has given us to create, with Jesus as carpenter, Jesus as King (a royalty theme).*

THEMED COLLAGES

a Christmas collages

• **Surprise collage** Using black or dark blue paper as a background, make a collage as follows: Prepare the background sheet by pasting areas of green paper on the lower half of the background for hills. Then cut along the edge of the hills in the centre as shown. Add shepherds and sheep figures to the hills, and silver and gold stars to the sky.

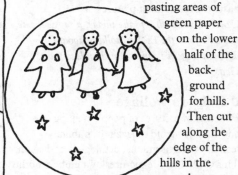

• **Cut circle from dark card.**
• **Pierce centre.**
• **Stick stars on one half, angels on the other.**
• **Assemble.**

Now cut a large circle from card, the diameter of the slit in the hills. Cover with dark paper or paint, and on one half paste stars and on the other half, angels. Attach to the background using a paper fastener so only

Cut

○
Pierce hole for paper fastener

• se black or dark • **Add shepherds and** • **Paste areas of green** • **Use adhesive stars or**
e card.   **sheep figures.**   **paper here.**   **silver foil.**

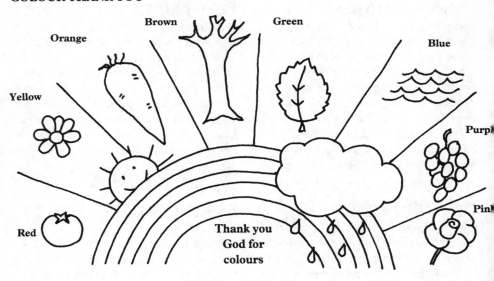

half shows at a time; the stars should be visible but not the angels, then when the circle is turned, the angels should appear.
• **Enjoying Christmas** Make a group collage focusing on the things we enjoy about Christmas. Provide magazines, catalogues, old Christmas cards and wrapping paper from which to cut out pictures of toys, trimmings, decorations, food, and so on. Paste these on to a background sheet headed, 'Things we like about Christmas'. Another option would be to cut out a manger or star from contrasting plain paper and paste on top of the collage, heading it 'The best thing about Christmas'.

USES for Christmas collages: *Link both collages with a Christmas theme.*

b Sharing collage

From magazine pictures, blank paper and colouring materials create a collage of things which can be shared, eg, food and toys, but also ears for listening, hands for helping, feet for running errands, and so on. Paste on to a large background sheet, shaped like a fruit and entitle it, 'Good gifts to share'.
USES: *Use with a sharing theme, or a theme which looks at our gifts and abilities. Help the children to realise that although they may not have a lot of material things, they have plenty of God-given gifts to share.*

c Praise collage

Cut out pictures of musical instruments from magazines or catalogues, or draw outlines for the children to colour in. Have the children draw around their hands and cut them out roughly. Then, at the bottom of the background sheet, paste one or more pairs of hands expressing praise. At the top, paste more hands in clapping positions. In between paste the instrument pictures.
USES: *Link with a praise theme, a music theme, passages from the Psalms, talking about the different ways we can use our hands to praise God.*

d Helpers' collage

Find lots of pictures of people helping one another, using old magazines, publicity leaflets, advertisements, catalogues and so on. This could include pictures of members of the 'caring professions', but also pictures of able-bodied and those with disabilities sharing activities, a child setting a meal table, a parent helping a child, an older child playing a game with a younger one, an adult helping a child to care for a sick pet. Paste all of these on to a background sheet with the caption, 'We do what is right when we help'.
USES: *Use with stories of people helping one another (eg, stories of Jesus, David and*

Mephibosheth, David and Abigail), linking with how we can help one another.

e Colour collages

• **Colour thank you** Draw a rainbow at the bottom of a large sheet of paper as shown above. Divide the rest of the paper into several sections according to the numbers of colours you want to use (not necessarily the colours of the rainbow). Label each section by colouring a circle with a felt-tipped pen, writing the colour name alongside if desired. Cut out lots of pictures from magazines which feature the various colours and paste in the correct colour section. Add a yellow sun, a white cloud, blue raindrops and the caption, 'Thank you, God, for colours'.
• **Rainbow collage** Draw a large rainbow outline on to card or heavy paper and cut into strips. Give individuals or small groups one colour of tissue paper each (corresponding to the colours of the rainbow) and let them screw up small bits and paste these on to their strip. When completed, assemble the rainbow on the wall.
USES: *Link with a theme on colours, using Bible stories which feature colour, such as Noah, gifts for the temple, Rahab's red cord, Lydia seller of purple cloth, furnishing the tabernacle, the priests' garments, and so on.*

TOPIC COLLAGES

a Fishing collages

• **Three men in a boat** Using the templates on the facing page, make individual or group collages of three fishermen in a boat, using blue paper for the background, and coloured sticky paper cut into the right shapes for the boat, the sail and the faces and bodies of the fishermen. Use the nets in which supermarkets package fruit and vegetables for the fishing net, and make fish from tin foil, shiny paper or tissue paper to go in the net. Assemble as shown.

• **Fishing boat** Enlarge the boat outline on the facing page and create a fishing collage as suggested.

USES for fishing collages: *Use with stories to do with Jesus and the disciples, eg, how Jesus called the fishermen, the amazing haul of fish, and so on.*

b Litter collage

Draw a picture of a rubbish bin on a large sheet of paper or card. Above this, paste plenty of sweet wrappers, crisp packets, pieces of newspaper, flattened cartons of fruit drinks – anything 'clean' that could be described as litter. When it is finished, paste two hand shapes on to the collage, positioned so that they appear to be throwing the litter in the bin.
USES: *Link with a theme to do with caring for God's world, a 'green' theme.*

c Garden collage

Draw or collage a patch of garden on a background sheet, using materials to represent bare soil only. Then cut pictures of flowers and trees from magazines, seed catalogues, old greetings cards, and so on. Let the children use their imaginations and their hands to create a colourful garden.
USES: *Link with a theme to do with how we care for God's world, pointing out that people who make gardens are using their hands to care for God's world. Link also with 'creating' and 'providing' themes from the Psalms.*

d Foot collage

Draw around one foot of each person in the group, including adults, to show that everyone can follow Jesus. Have them write their name on their footprint. You should have a fairly equal number of left and right footprints. On a large sheet of coloured paper, draw or paste a picture of Jesus in the top left-hand corner. Cut out the shapes and paste

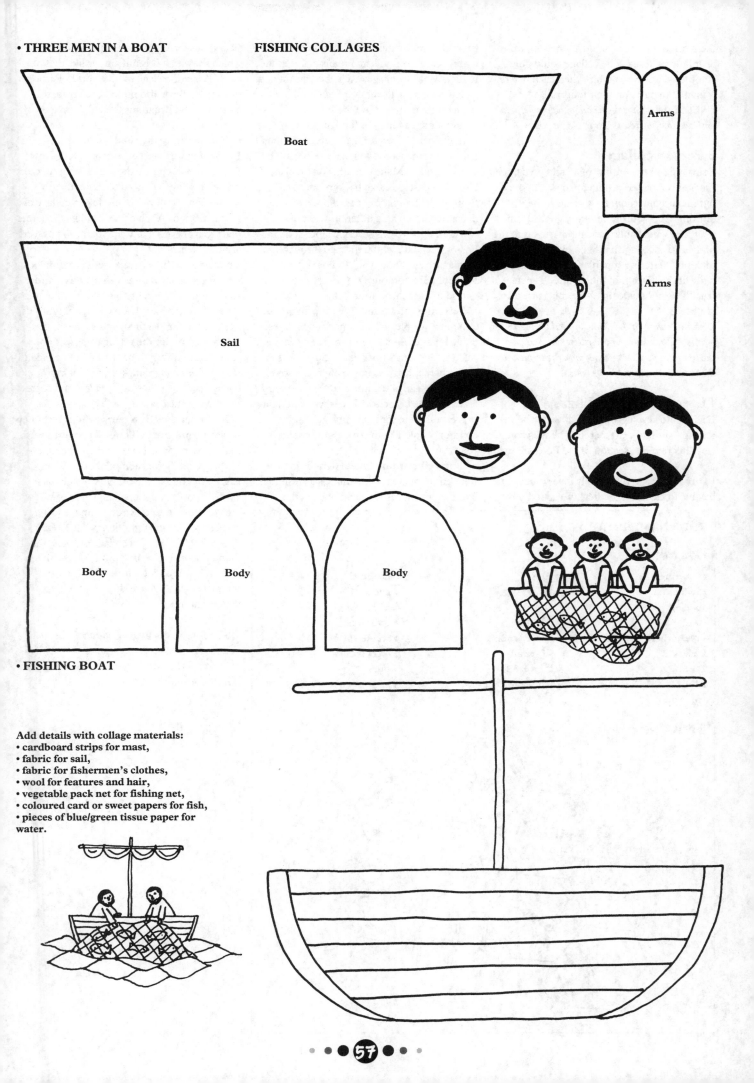

• THREE MEN IN A BOAT   FISHING COLLAGES

Boat

Arms

Arms

Sail

Body

Body

Body

• FISHING BOAT

Add details with collage materials:
• cardboard strips for mast,
• fabric for sail,
• fabric for fishermen's clothes,
• wool for features and hair,
• vegetable pack net for fishing net,
• coloured card or sweet papers for fish,
• pieces of blue/green tissue paper for water.

them on to the background so they appear to be following Jesus. The collage could be completed during worship when each person is invited to paste on their footprint.

USES: *Link with a theme on following Jesus, with the story of Jesus calling the disciples.*

e Person collage

Draw around the outline of a child on a large sheet of wallpaper or lining paper. Cut out the outline, leaving room for a verse at the bottom. Cut pictures of luxury goods from magazines and catalogues and paste on to the body until a collage has been built up. Finally, in outline lettering suitable for colouring in, write at the bottom of the picture, 'A person's true life is not made up of the things he owns' (Luke 12:15).

USES: *Link with the theme of God providing for our needs, the theme of priorities, stories such as the parable of the rich young fool, the sermon on the mount, Solomon, and so on.*

f Lord's Prayer collages

Divide into seven groups, each with a helper and appropriate craft materials. Each group can illustrate one section of the Lord's Prayer as follows:

• **Our Father in heaven** It is very special to be able to call God 'Father'. We can do this because Jesus invites us to be part of his family. God loves to listen to his children talk to him. Make a collage; each child cutting out a picture of herself with a speech bubble saying something to God the Father.

• **Your name is holy** 'Holy' means that God is very special. Everything about him is good. Think of some words which describe how special God is. Make a 'patchwork' collage: hexagons pasted onto a background (see 'Let's make templates', page 95), each one decorated and with a different word of worship, or words to describe God. It might be fun with older children to go through the alphabet: Lord God, you're Amazing, Brilliant, Creator, our Dad, Everywhere ... and so on (see illustration below).

• **Your kingdom come** We pray that more and more people will become friends of Jesus and be part of God's family or kingdom. Jesus said that his kingdom is like a mustard seed that grows and grows into a big mustard tree. Make a collage of the mustard tree with birds sitting on the branches. The leaves could have prayers on them for the people whom the children would like to see become friends of Jesus.

• **Your will be done on earth as it is in heaven** In heaven, everything is as it should be. Everyone loves God and one another.

Everyone worships God. Think of situations which show that it is not always like that on earth. Make a collage of 'the world'. Paste prayers for the world on to it, referring to countries and situations the children know about.

• **Give us today the food we need** Everything we have comes from God. How does our food come from him? What food do we need today? We need to remember to thank God for all we have. Make a collage of favourite foods (each child could have a paper plate to work on) and write thank you prayers around them.

• **Forgive us the wrongs we have done as we forgive the wrongs others have done to us** We all do wrong things from time to time, and other people do wrong things to us. We need to forgive them and we need to say 'sorry' to God for the wrong things *we* do. Jesus didn't do anything wrong but he died to forgive the wrong things we do. Make a collage cross, write 'sorry' prayers and paste them on to the cross.

• **Do not lead us into temptation, but keep us safe from the evil one** When Jesus was in the desert for forty days praying to his Father, God, he was tempted to do wrong things, but he said, 'No'. He will help us to say 'No' too, if we keep close to him. When are we tempted to do wrong things? (Sing 'When we find the right things hard', *Let's Join In!* p119). Make a collage of Jesus, the Good Shepherd. Write prayers on the sheep shapes (use templates from 'Let's make templates' page 85), asking God to keep us close to him.

USES for Lord's Prayer collages: *Use to illustrate the meanings of the various sections of the Lord's Prayer and to provide opportunities for further discussion.*

YOUR NAME IS HOLY

Lord God, you're

Amazing	**J**udge	**S**hepherd
Brilliant	**K**ing	**T**eacher
Caring	**L**ove	**U**nchanging
Dad	**M**ighty	**V**ictorious
Everywhere	**N**ever ending	**W**onderful
Friend	**O**ver all	**EX**tra special
Great	**P**owerful	**Y**ourself
Holy	**Q**uick to hear us	**A and Z** – first and last
Important	**R**ock	

A patchwork collage

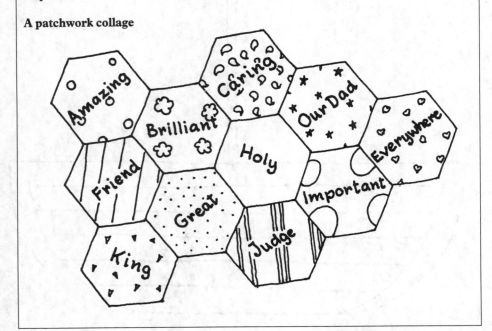

● POSTERS

POSTER STYLES

a Using shapes

• **People** Make cut-out figures with the words 'I can ...', written on them, and have the children add suggestions for ways in which they can help. Paste these on to a large sheet of paper with the heading, 'We can help ...'.
USES: *Link with the theme of offerings to God, the theme of helping; tie in with a prayer and worship time. The figures could be used to illustrate any number of themes to do with our response as individuals.*

• **Trees** Make tree shapes and arrange on a sheet of paper to make a collage. Alternatively, make stencils from the shapes for the children to paint.
USES: *Use with a materials theme, with a theme to do with strength or shelter, with a provision theme.*

b Using theme-related materials

On a large poster write the words, 'Jesus has come' and decorate using shiny paper, tinsel, stars, glitter and so on – materials traditionally associated with Christmas.
USES: *Use in a Christmas Day display; use other materials to link with different themes: flowers, coloured cotton wool balls (to represent lambs), fresh greenery for Easter; dried grasses and leaves, pulses, ripe fruits for harvest or autumn; wind, fire and dove elements for Pentecost, and so on.*

c Coloured lettering

Using outline lettering and lower case letters, write theme-related messages on large sheets of paper, such as 'Jesus is our friend' or 'God loves us'. Use squares of coloured paper to fill in the letters, then cut the letters out when completed and mount on a large poster.
USES: *Use to highlight particular truths for the children to remember: promises, 'I am' statements, theme verses, and so on, talking about the message as the children work on it.*

d Picture posters

Use cut-out pictures or draw pictures to illustrate a particular theme, then paste on to an appropriate background. For example, cut items from magazines regarded as 'treasure', paste in a treasure-chest shaped poster with a hinged lid. Lift the lid to read, 'The Kingdom of God: worth selling all these to gain it!'.

Another idea is to paste pictures of boats on a wavy sea background, to lead in to talking about boats, and Jesus and the fishermen.
USES: *Pictures may be linked with any theme or story, as discussion starters, in worship, for prayer and so on.*

DOOR POSTER

Prepare a large sheet of heavy paper as a background. Across the top in outline lettering for colouring in write, 'What do we tell people about Jesus?' Below it paste on another length of paper with five or six doors on it, cut on three sides so as to open. Behind the door write/draw things we can tell: 'He came to earth', 'He is the Lord', 'He wants us to be kind', 'He loves us' and so on. Decorate the doors and the rest of the poster, adding paper fasteners for door handles.
USES: *Link with any theme to emphasise a series, eg, 'What did God create?', 'What did Jesus teach us about light?', 'God's special promises are ...'.*

HANDS AND FEET POSTERS

Mix up a quantity of powder paint in a flat pan (for feet or hands), or alternatively soak a wad of paper towels in paint to make a printing pad (for hands). Roll out a strip of paper along the floor and let the children step into the pan then straight on to the paper to make footprints. Then, when dry write 'Jesus said, "Follow me"', in amongst the footprints. Make a poster of handprints as shown, writing words in the centre of the circle. Have available washing-up bowls of soapy water, towels, and for the foot painting, plastic tablecloths or equivalent. A less messy approach is to draw around feet and hands, cut out and paste on to the poster.
USES: *Link with themes to do with following, using our hands for God, our bodies, and so on.*

INFORMATION POSTERS

Produce a selection of posters inviting people to join special services or events at your church. Include information about times and places. For speed these could be ready-printed on A3 or A4 sheets, with a design or picture for the children to colour in. Place on the church notice-board, and ask children in nearby houses or children whose parents own a shop to display posters in a front window. Smaller versions could be taken home for information.
USES: *Use for advertising purposes; help the children to 'own' an event relevant to them by being involved in promoting it.*

10 Let's make books

shapes out of contrasting paper and paste these on the inside pages, one on the first page, two on the next and so on until the five pages are completed, then assemble the book and staple.

USES: *The book can be used to represent God's family and those who visit it. The figures inside can be named and talked about as representing various groups within the church.*

c House books

You will need two sheets of A4 paper, folded top to bottom, stapled on the left and cut to resemble a house. The children can colour in or paste windows and a door on the front cover. Inside they can paste in pictures appropriate to the various rooms of the house, cut from catalogues or advertisements. They could also draw in people.

USES: *These can link with themes to do with families, homes, belonging, and so on.*

D o you think of books as lots of words printed on page after page of paper, folded over and bound in a cover? Well, think again, because there are many different styles of books in this section and not one of them fits that description!

Here you will find books with windows, books that roll up, books shaped like houses, books that stand up, books that hang up – books that are fun to make, fun to use, fun to share, fun to take home. It is never too early to introduce children to different types of books, to help them think about how books come into being and what sorts of things can go into books. The books in this section can be large and created together as a group (floor books) or they can be smaller and worked on individually ('about me' books). They can be linked to a particular story or topic, used to encourage prayer, used to record a special event – the limit is your imagination!

Don't forget that younger children especially like to be able to take home a project that they have worked on. Often group projects are retained for display or for use in later weeks. You may choose to make individual books for taking home – or how about photographing parts of the group project and mounting the photos in a special frame to take home? It could even be a gift.

In the next few pages, you will find a number of basic book styles followed by books which are focused around particular topics.

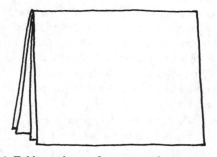

1. Fold two sheets of paper together.

• BASIC BOOK STYLES

SHAPE BOOKS
a People books
b Our church
c House books

ZIGZAG BOOKS

SCRAP-BOOKS

WINDOW BOOKS

SCROLLS
a Miniature scrolls
b Simple scrolls

FLOOR BOOK

FLICK BOOK

PHOTO BOOK

• TOPIC BOOKS

DAY AND NIGHT BOOKS

THANK YOU BOOK

PRAYER BOOKS
a Please, sorry and thank you
b Church family prayers

BOOKS ABOUT ME
a Concertina book
b Folded books

2. Staple left edge. Cut roof to form house shape.
Let child draw windows and door.

3. Glue in pictures.

• BASIC BOOK STYLES

SHAPE BOOKS

a People books

Make a template of a person facing sideways, so that the person's back runs down the centre fold of the book. Sew or staple additional pages into the book as required.

USES: *Link with a theme of 'Who am I?' using*

the pages to illustrate 'What I enjoy doing'. Link with a Bible character or with Jesus, including pictures of various events in the person's life.

b Our church

Make a template (A4 size) in the shape of your church building or meeting place. Using this, cut two card covers and five coloured pages for each book. Cut people

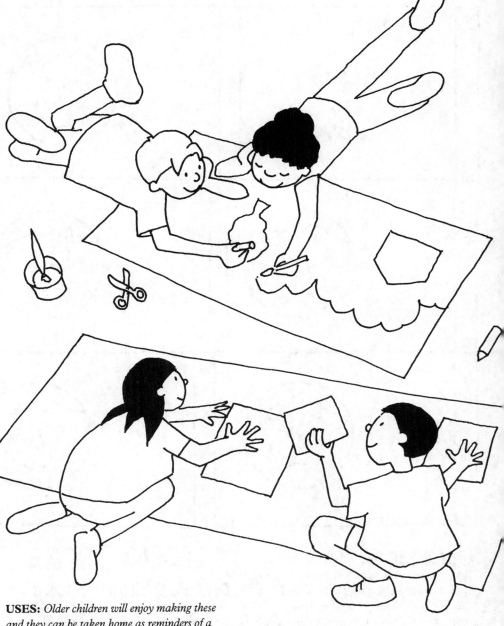

ZIGZAG BOOKS

Concertina-fold a long rectangle of stiff paper to make half a dozen panels. Stand the book on a table horizontally or hang vertically on the wall. Paste a card panel on the front and back covers for added strength.

USES: *This book could be used to illustrate a series of story scenes, to make a frieze, to draw pictures of people to pray for … the uses are unlimited.*

SCRAP-BOOKS

Use large sheets of sugar paper folded in half and held together with a couple of strong stitches, staples, or punched with two holes and threaded with thick plaited wool which can be tied in a bow. A card cover will make it more durable.

USES: *As these are large books and the paper is thick, they are ideal for group projects involving cutting and sticking.*

WINDOW BOOKS

Lay four sheets of paper on top of each other and draw a picture on the top sheet (eg, a boat with Jesus and the disciples). Choose an interesting part of the picture and cut around it to make a window (eg, Jesus). Through the window, draw in the missing part of the picture on the second sheet, then draw a different picture on the second sheet around the picture of Jesus (eg, Jesus healing someone). Choose an interesting part of this picture and cut around it to make another small window, drawing the missing part on to the third sheet and so on.

USES: *These books are quite fiddly for young children to make, but make good visual aids for a story and the children enjoy guessing what will come next. Older children will enjoy the challenge of making them.*

USES: *Older children will enjoy making these and they can be taken home as reminders of a particular story or verse.*

SCROLLS

a Miniature scrolls
Follow the diagram to make miniature scrolls.

b Simple scrolls
Use long strips of paper to form scrolls, rolling them up from both ends. Roll around pencils or lengths of dowelling which can be fixed in with sticky tape or removed once the paper is well rolled. The children can write, draw and enjoy rolling and unrolling their scrolls.

USES: *Use to illustrate how writing used to be done, how the Bible was written and as a story visual aid.*

FLOOR BOOK

Prepare a number of large sheets of paper (lining paper or wallpaper is ideal). Plan out the contents of the book as a large group, then divide into pairs or smaller groups and have each illustrate and decorate one page. When completed, staple, sew or paste the pages together.

USES: *This is ideal for a group activity to illustrate a theme or a story and to experience working co-operatively together towards a common goal. These books make very effective display material.*

HOW TO MAKE A MINIATURE SCROLL

You will need:
two cotton buds,
a length of brown paper
(an old envelope will do!),
scissors,
paste,
thread,
a dark brown and a black
felt-tip pen.

• Colour the two cotton buds black, then paste one to either end of the paper.

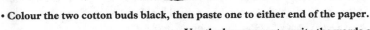

• Use the brown pen to write the words of this week's memory verse.

• Then roll up the scroll and tie it with a length of thread.

• Cut along the bold lines and assemble with picture 1 on top.

FLICK BOOK

Prepare a small 'booklet' of sheets of paper which can be held in the left hand and 'flicked' with the right hand to show movement through a progression of pictures, eg, sad to happy. Younger children are helped by having the sheets graded to make 'flicking' easier (see illustration above), while older children can manage their own flicking if the sheets are kept level.

USES: *This is a fun way of demonstrating movement, eg, Jesus healing the paralysed man; in the first picture he is lying down and in the last he is jumping. Pictures are best kept simple without too much detail.*

PHOTO BOOK

Use personal photograph albums to introduce a particular topic, eg, pets, family, holidays, or take pictures as a group and put together your own album. Talk about how you take the pictures, how you choose which ones to include, how you arrange them in the album, etc.

USES: *Use to introduce a particular topic, or to give an idea, at a simple level, of how a book comes into being.*

● TOPIC BOOKS

DAY AND NIGHT BOOKS

Fold an A4 piece of coloured card in half. On the front put a picture of the sun rising. Inside, the children can paste or draw pictures of anything relating to 'morning' activities, eg, favourite breakfast cereal, an alarm clock, cleaning teeth.

Fold plain paper into a small book and staple or punch and thread with wool. On the front write, '[Name's] bedtime book'. Inside the children can draw or paste pictures of things associated with bedtime.

USES: *These books help to reinforce the truth that Jesus is with us at all times of the day and night.*

THANK YOU BOOK

Contribute as group members to a large book which says 'thank you' to God. As the Bible is God's letter to us, encourage the children to write or draw thank you letters back to God. Encourage 'praise' and 'thank you' aspects rather than 'asking' ones – the book should be a celebration.

PRAYER BOOKS

a Please, sorry and thank you

Compile sheets of paper on these three themes: 'Please' – ask the children what they would like to ask God for, write these out and illustrate; 'Sorry' – write out a number of typical situations, talk about them and draw out the point that 'sorry' needs to be said, then let the children decorate the pieces of paper; 'Thank you' – let the children draw things which they enjoy and want to thank God for. Gather the sheets together and make them into a book.

USES: *Use when praying together during a worship-time.*

b Church family prayers

Make a group book about all those who serve in the church. On each page, draw a picture of a person who helps and write the person's name and job. Sew the pages together with wool, or staple.

USES: *Use to help the children become aware of the wider church family, of unseen jobs that need doing, of what it means to 'serve' and 'help'.*

BOOKS ABOUT ME

a Concertina book

Make concertina (or zigzag) books as shown above, photocopying outlines and allowing individual children to complete the details.

USES: *Use to help children think about their growing bodies, about being well and healthy, recognising that we can thank God for good health, thinking also about those who are not well or who have disabilities.*

b Folded books

Make simple books as shown here, allowing younger children to fill in as much as possible on their own, giving help where needed.

USES: *This will help children focus on the fact that books may be written so we can know more about people – linking with books in the Bible.*

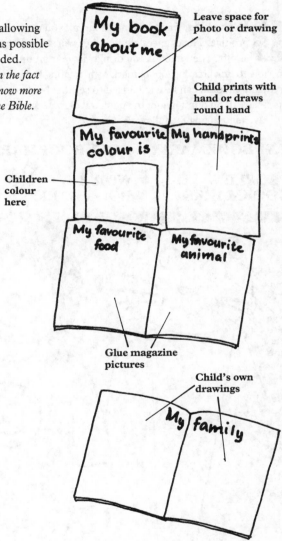

11 Let's make bookmarks

'Bookmarks are fine for some children,' you may say, 'but my group don't read.' Think positive! The chances are that they will still enjoy making them and they can be given as gifts, used in books on display in your group, or used to mark a Bible story. It is also possible to link creating a bookmark with creating books (see 'Let's make books', page 60) and gradually children can be encouraged to see that books open up a much wider world than at first realised. So don't ignore the potential of this section.

Have fun making the following:

CAT BOOKMARK   **BOAT BOOKMARK**   **GENERAL BOOKMARKS**

PEOPLE BOOKMARKS   **WORM BOOKMARK**

Triangles of pink card.

Large white circles, pupils crayoned in.

Use artstraws or strips of white card for whiskers.

God knows all about me

CAT BOOKMARK
Cut a rectangle of card, 18-20 cm long for the body and round off bottom corners. Cut a tail from black paper to paste to the bottom of the body and a cat's head with ears to paste to the top. Add details as shown.
USES: *Use with a theme on books or animals, or give as a gift.*

PEOPLE BOOKMARKS
Cut card in the shape of gingerbread people. Thread several strands of plaited wool or embroidery thread through a hole punched in

the top, tying the ends to make a simple tassel. On one side write a verse such as Psalm 139:1-2 or 'God knows all about me' and on the reverse the child can write about herself or draw a picture of herself.

USES: *Use different verses to fit with your theme or story and use different shapes as appropriate.*

BOAT BOOKMARK

Write a verse on the boat shape. Cut a wave and attach to the boat with a paper fastener, moving the wave to read the verse.

USES: *Use as a memory verse reminder to pop into a book.*

WORM BOOKMARK

Using the picture opposite as a template, draw a bookworm on card, then colour in the body with stripes or paint and decorate with self-adhesive stars or spots.

USES: *Make as a present for family or a friend, showing that being generous involves giving (time, effort and thought).*

GENERAL BOOKMARKS

Prepare strips of stiff paper (wallpaper) or card. 'Fringe' both ends with scissors and/or paste on shapes of attractive paper.

USES: *Take home as a gift, or use to mark pages of special interest in books on display.*

The Lord stayed with me and gave me strength.

2 Timothy 4:17

Paper fastener

Wave shape to cover verse

12 Let's make mobiles

using sticky tape and then tape the other end of the wool to a coat-hanger. Each child can produce one mobile showing her family members.

USES for family mobiles: *Link with a family theme – extended and nuclear families (pets are also important here); link with belonging to God's family/church/world-wide family.*

WEATHER MOBILE

Enlarge weather symbols (see weather symbols in 'Let's make templates', page 93) and cut out a number of each for colouring. Tape to, or hang from, a length of string to decorate the room, or assemble to make individual mobiles hung from a garden cane.

USES: *Link with Bible stories which have a weather theme, eg, Noah, storm on the lake, wise and foolish builders; also link with a creation theme or with God as provider for his world.*

L ook above a baby's cot, in a child's bedroom, in a school classroom. Chances are you will see a mobile of some description and even the simplest of mobiles can be fun to look at, colourful and imaginative. The term 'mobile' (as used in this section) also covers individual hanging items such as the stuffed fish, although technically, a mobile is a series of hanging items which are balanced against each other and so achieve an equilibrium. One of the frustrations with mobiles is that they never seem to balance properly. A simple rule of thumb to help achieve a correct balance is to move an item on the 'down' side nearer to the centre balance point. Once a correct balance has been achieved, items can then be taped or glued into position.

In making a mobile, long or short garden canes make ideal cross-pieces from which to hang items. They can be left plain or bound with coloured tape (eg, insulating tape) or crêpe paper. Though less attractive, coat-hangers can also be decorated and used; care should be taken that sharp wire ends are covered with thick tape. While they can be made individually, mobiles also make ideal group projects and can encourage team-work and co-operation.

Try some of the following:

CREATION MOBILES

a Sun, moon and stars

For the sun, blow up a large yellow or orange balloon. Dab with glue and shake over some gold glitter or pieces of bright yellow paper. For the moon, use a white balloon and cover with pieces of silver foil and white paper. Cut big star shapes and cover with silver foil. Hang from two crossed lengths of bamboo cane.

USES: *Link with a creation theme, talking about how big the sun, moon and stars actually*

FAMILY MOBILES
a Houses
b Faces

WEATHER MOBILE

CREATION MOBILES
a Sun, moon and stars
b Creation spirals

FRIEND MOBILE

ALL STARS MOBILE

DOVE MOBILES
a Peace mobile
b Hanging dove

PENTECOST MOBILE

RAINBOW MOBILE

FISH MOBILES
a Pleated fish
b Fish shapes

SHEEP MOBILE

GOD'S WORLD MOBILE

GROWING THINGS MOBILE

CREATION SPIRALS

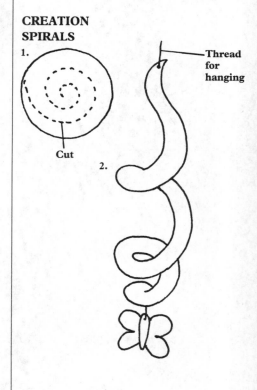

1.

Cut

2.

Thread for hanging

FAMILY MOBILES

a Houses

Cut house-shaped outlines from paper or card and write, 'Jesus welcomes families' on one side of each. On the other side, children can draw pictures of their family group. Punch a hole in the top, thread with wool and attach to garden canes.

b Faces

Draw and colour in individual family members on ovals of card. Each child can draw as many as she wishes. Younger children can be helped by drawing simple faces or figures for them to colour in. On the back, attach each oval to a length of wool

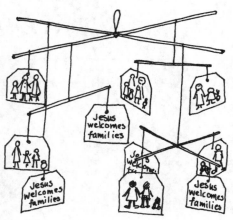

FRIEND MOBILE

Draw faces of friends on circles of card, then thread on to wool or thin string and hang from a coat-hanger or garden cane.

USES: *Link with a friendship theme, the fun we can have with friends and how friends can share and play together.*

ALL STARS MOBILE

Follow the illustration opposite to create a star mobile, making the stars from bright yellow, gold or foil-covered card. Write words, such as those shown, on the front and the back. Make large stars for a group project, or smaller stars for individual mobiles.

USES: *Link with a theme stressing the truth that each person is infinitely precious to God; alternately change the words to link with a Christmas theme or a creation theme, etc.*

Front   Back

Jesus cares for.. / everyone!
Jesus listens to.. / everyone!
Jesus welcomes / everyone!
We're all stars.. / ..to Jesus!

are, although looking small to us. Link with a power theme, thinking of the power of the sun and of God's greatness as creator.

b Creation spirals

Make spiral mobiles (as shown) decorating each with cut-out pictures of the sun, stars, butterflies, birds, etc. Hang individually or in groups from a wire coat-hanger or similar frame. A saucer makes a useful spiral template.

USES: *Use when talking about God's wonderful creation. Separate mobiles could be topic-linked: birds, animals, sea creatures, etc.*

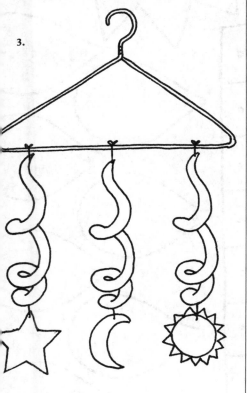

3.

DOVE MOBILES

a Peace mobile

Cut dove shapes from thin card as illustrated (see also 'Let's make templates', page 90), making a small slit in the side of the bird. Pleat a piece of paper very finely, insert through the slit and fan out on either side for wings. Attach each bird to a different length of string or shirring elastic and hang from a piece of card with 'peace' written on it.

USES: *Link with a peace theme, perhaps from the minor prophets, or from Jesus' teachings; alternatively, change the word and link with a theme on the Holy Spirit.*

b Hanging dove

Make doves from thin white card as shown in the illustration and colour in a beak and eye on each side. Write a verse or phrase linked with the story or theme around the base of the bird, then cut a slit 2 mm wide in the side of each bird, using a craft knife. Pleat a rectangle of paper, slot through the slit and fan out for wings. Make several and tie to different lengths of string, then hang in a group, eg, attached to a circular card strip.

USES: *Link with the story of Jesus' baptism or the Holy Spirit; or omit (or change) the verse and link with a creation, wind, or travelling theme.*

PENTECOST MOBILE

Write the words of a verse to do with the Holy Spirit on to a long strip of card (eg, 'The Holy Spirit ... will teach you everything', John 14:26), then join the ends to make a circle. Cut out and colour in three dove and three flame shapes, thread on to different lengths of string and attach to the circle. Hang the circle in a breeze.

USES: *Link with Holy Spirit/Pentecost theme: the dove and flame shapes are blown by the wind, thus illustrating the three symbols representing the Holy Spirit.*

RAINBOW MOBILE

Example of finished mobile.

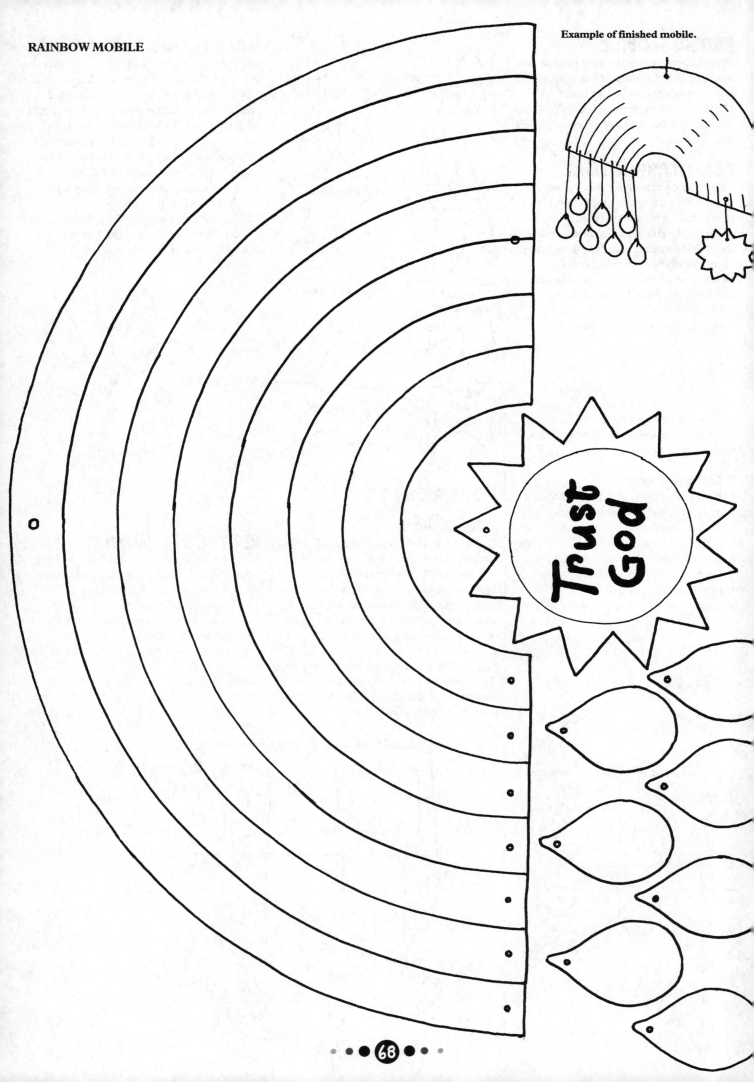

Trust God

RAINBOW MOBILE

Reproduce the rainbow, sun and raindrops from the template on page 68 on to thin white card, colour in and assemble as shown.

USES: *Link with the story of Noah, with God's promises to us and the theme of trust, with a creation theme.*

FISH MOBILES

a Pleated fish

Cut out fish shapes from coloured paper, or colour them separately, then pleat as shown and hang from a cardboard fish template to make a mobile.

USES: *This activity can link with any of the fishing stories in the Gospels; a verse or title could be written on the big fish.*

b Fish shapes

Make two large fish shapes, copying the illustration, then colour brightly. When finished, stuff with newspaper and staple together. (Ensure you colour the correct sides of the fish for backing together.) Make a large number of different sizes of fish like this and suspend from the ceiling to make a colourful display.

USES: *Link with any fishing theme.*

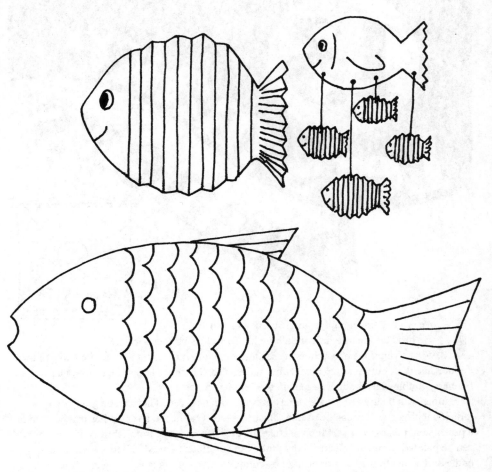

SHEEP MOBILE

Using a sheep template (see 'Let's make templates', pages 89–91), cut out two sheep from card and cover with cotton wool, colouring in the head and legs. Tape a length of string or wool to the back of one sheep, thread through a strong plastic straw and

attach the end to the second sheep. Move the string back and forth through the straw to achieve the correct balance. Attach a shape to the centre of the straw, write on it an appropriate verse and hang up the mobile from the centre of the straw.

USES: *This activity can link with a sheep theme (Jesus' stories, Psalm 23), or replace the sheep with other animals or objects, select a suitable verse and link with other themes.*

GOD'S WORLD MOBILE

Provide circles of card (approx. 20 cm in diameter). On one side draw or paste on pictures cut from magazines showing 'God's beautiful world'. On the reverse draw or paste pictures to show 'God's spoilt world'. Sweet wrappers, can rings, newspaper scraps, graffiti, pictures of war and of hungry people could be used. Make a hole at the top of the circle, thread string through and hang up.

USES: *Link with a theme on caring for God's world, suffering, environmental issues, and so on; or use the mobile style as a basis for depicting two other contrasting issues.*

GROWING THINGS MOBILE

Draw or paint pictures of growing things (including people). Cut around these, mount on card and draw a border (or mount on coloured paper) and attach each picture to a wire coat-hanger. Add words such as 'Thank you, God'.

USES: *Use as a visual prayer; alter the pictures and words to link with any theme or story.*

13 Let's make banners

'Love is a flag flown high from the castle of my heart ...'
'He brought me into his banqueting house and his banner over me is love ...'
What's your idea of a banner? A rectangle of cloth hung from a pole? Well, lots of them do look like that, but there are many other styles, also. There are lollipop banners, flag banners, double-sided banners – look in the next few pages!

Banners can be used in a wide variety of ways with children. They can be group or individual projects; they can be used to illustrate a story, a theme, a verse; they can be used in a procession, in songs, in worship, in a display; they can be made from fabric or paper; they can be painted, printed, collaged, sewn; they can be colour-themed ... The variations are endless! Best of all, they do not need to be complicated to be effective – in fact, some of the simplest are the most striking. This means even the youngest children can be involved.

So dip into the next few pages and have some fun.

d Flag banners
Make simple flag-style banners about a metre long from stiff paper or card, cut in a flag shape and attached to bamboo canes or a length of dowelling. Draw or write on them and colour in.
USES: *These can be used in a similar way to the lollipop banners, but are quicker to make.*

e Mini banners
Using sheets of A4 paper (or strips of lining paper), sticky tape, and garden canes or sticks to hold each side, make mini banners which can be held in two hands by one child. Prepare ahead of time with outline lettering for younger children to colour in and decorate. Older children can design their own.
USES: *Use to highlight the main points drawn out from a story or a theme, eg, facts about God for which we can praise him, praise phrases, words of a song, and so on.*

f Maxi banners
Use strong paper, 100 cm wide by 60 cm deep, and two pieces of dowelling or broom

LOLLIPOP BANNERS

BANNER STYLES	USING FABRIC	c 'Friends of God' banner
a Using letters	a 'Jesus is alive' banner	d Elijah banner
b Using buttons	b Easter banner	e Trinity banner
c Lollipop banners	c Angel banner	
d Flag banners	d Jesus banner	**USING FABRIC**
e Mini banners	e Fabric banners	**OR PAPER**
f Maxi banners		a Friends of Jesus
g Double-sided banner	**USING PAPER**	b Pentecost
	a Justice banner	c Advent banners
	b Christmas banners	d Jesus is light

BANNER STYLES

a Using letters
Write each letter of a phrase or verse (eg, 'Trust in the Lord') on to a separate A4 sheet of stiff paper or thin card. Write in outline or hollow lettering and make each letter the same size. Colour in the letters then cut out and staple in the correct order to a length of string or cord and hang up against a wall. The letters could also be filled in with scrunched up tissue balls, in mosaic fashion, or by painting. This is ideal for younger children as it does not require a lot of fiddly work.
USES: *Use as a story reminder, to highlight a theme, to focus on a verse, and so on.*

b Using buttons
On a large piece of stiff paper or fabric, print a phrase or verse (eg, 'Thank you, Lord, for

friends'). Provide a collection of buttons and threaded needles and have the children (one or two at a time to prevent needles going astray) sew buttons close together over the printing to make the message stand out. Visit jumble sales or charity shops to collect buttons.
USES: *Use in making a banner of a more permanent nature, eg, highlighting a series' theme, a seasonal banner, a group name, or as part of a larger banner.*

c Lollipop banners
Make large round individual banners from card and broom handles as shown opposite.
USES: *Use to highlight a series of items (eg, the days of creation, 'I am' sayings of Jesus, the seasons, praise shouts) using drawings and/or writing; use in displays, marches, processions around the church.*

handles to attach to either side. Roll the ends of the paper around the dowelling and secure with parcel tape.

USES: *Make together as a group project to highlight a theme or story, eg, paste a globe or small world map in the centre surrounded by cut-out pictures of children and write 'Jesus said, "Let the children come to me"', at the top. Use in worship time, as a church display, and so on.*

g Double-sided banner

Make a two-sided banner as shown opposite using fabric, felt and dowelling rods at the top and bottom. On one side have a question and on the reverse, the answer.

USES: *Use to reinforce a theme or truth that has been discussed, eg, 'Decide today who you will serve' and 'I will serve the Lord'; 'Why am I so troubled?' and 'I will put my hope in God'.*

Front — Dowelling rod top and bottom — Mountain shape — Waves

Is anything TOO HARD for the LORD?

Back — Cord and tassels attached — Cut out THICK letters from felt. Glue in place.

Everything is possible with GOD

USING FABRIC

a 'Jesus is alive!' banner

In the centre of a sheet or large piece of fabric, write or paint 'Jesus is alive!'. Around this, the children can make a circle of handprints and/or footprints (print directly on to the fabric using paint, or draw on paper, colour, cut out and attach with PVA glue). Make a second circle of butterfly (or animal) shapes, coloured in, then cut out and pasted on. Add a third circle of flower (or plant) shapes.

USES: *Use as an Easter display, talking while you work about flowers, animals and ourselves being alive, and reading the caption together.*

b Easter banner

Make a banner as illustrated below, using an old sheet or large piece of fabric for the background. Use different shades of blue

material for the clouds, orange or yellow material for the sun, and gold or yellow cord for the sun's rays. Use felt or fabric pens for the words. (NB The same design could be made on paper using collage techniques.)
USES: *Use as an Easter display banner.*

c Angel banner

Cut figures of angels (see 'Let's make templates' on page 94) from gold, yellow, or white felt (or other non-fraying material) and decorate by sewing or glueing on sequins and glitter. Stitch or paste angels to a dark blue or black fabric (or paper) background. The words, 'Glory to God', could also be cut from felt and added.
USES: *Use to display in your room or the church as a reminder of the joyful message the angels brought.*

d Jesus banner

Using a large piece of sheeting and fabric paints or pens, write the name JESUS in the centre of the banner. Then add other names given for Jesus as shown, positioning them at angles around the edge of the banner. Use bright colours and decorate liberally with sequins and beads for added glitter. Before making the banner, sew a seam along the top and bottom so that dowelling or bamboo poles can be inserted at the end. Attach a length of ribbon for hanging. (NB For speed and simplicity, a similar banner can be made using paint and marker pens and a strip of lining or wallpaper.)
USES: *Use as a worship banner to focus on during a praise and prayer session.*

e Fabric banners

Visit jumble sales to find plain-coloured cloth which can be cut to the size 20 x 30 cm. The banners can be painted in bold colours by the children or they could stick fabric shapes on to them, cut from patterned fabric. Attach with staples to a piece of garden cane, ensuring that the staple ends are covered with tape.
USES: *Use with younger children who will enjoy waving them in a praise march or procession.*

JESUS SAID I HAVE COME IN ORDER THAT YOU MIGHT HAVE LIFE JOHN 10:10

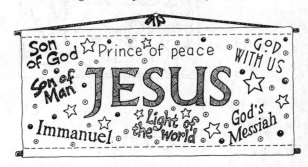

Son of God · Prince of peace · GOD WITH US · Son of Man · JESUS · Immanuel · the Light of the world · God's Messiah

Let justice flow like a river and righteousness like a stream that never goes dry. Amos 5:24

USING PAPER

a Justice banner

Provide slips of paper (15 cm long) and write 'justice' on half of them and 'righteousness' on the other half. Cut rolls of blue and white crêpe paper into long strips (each strip should be the full length of the roll). Unroll each strip. Using a green or pale blue background, secure the blue and white strips alternately at the top right of the background. Stretch them out across the banner and twist them individually, securing each one at the opposite end, spreading them out to look like a widening river. Use green paper to make a grassy riverbank with reeds and bulrushes. Staple the words on to the river at random, and write the words of Amos 5:24 at the bottom as shown above.

USES: *Use to illustrate the verse and for display when thinking about issues of justice and righteousness.*

b Christmas banners

Make simple but effective Christmas banners as shown below, using heavy paper and a length of garden cane. Write the caption in outline lettering for the children to colour or fill in as desired.

USES: *Link with the theme of who Jesus is and use in a Christmas display.*

Stick

Heavy paper

• Children draw pictures of themselves and paste them around the manger.

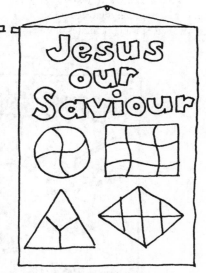

• For the manger:

Pink sticky paper

Yellow sticky paper

Brown sticky paper

• Children draw around their hands, cut out and paste the outlines on to the banner, ensuring fingers are free to move.

• Choose four Christmas cards depicting the Christmas story. Cut into jigsaws. Children reassemble and paste on to banner.

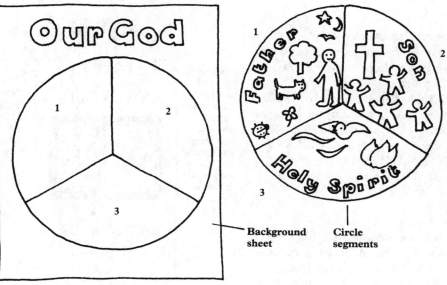

Background sheet   **Circle segments**

c 'Friends of God' banner

Produce a banner (as illustrated) which can be completed over a series of sessions. Use a long strip of lining paper for the background and roll around a piece of dowelling for hanging. Write in the words using marker pens. For the first section, cut out, write in and paste on the speech bubble. Have the children draw pictures of themselves on circles of paper, then paste these on together with their names. For the second section, write on characteristics of the children themselves. For the third section, draw around one foot of each child and paste on overlapping. For the final section cut out paper chain people and paste on around a larger Jesus figure.

USES: *Use to illustrate the theme of coming to Jesus; link with the idea of being part of a family; link with the theme that God accepts everyone.*

d Elijah banner

Have ready cut out the letters of the words, 'God never lets us down', to be coloured in and pasted on to the centre of a large background strip of lining paper. Older children can draw pictures from the Elijah stories on to separate sheets of paper and paste around the words. Younger children can do potato printing around the edges. Cut the potatoes to resemble roughly items from the stories, eg, bird, bread, jar of oil, flame.

USES: *Link with the stories of any Bible character, adapting the caption to suit the character, eg, 'God has a plan for each of us' for the story of Joseph.*

e Trinity banner

Prepare a large background sheet from card or stiff paper as shown above. In three groups prepare the three circle segments:
• Father – pictures to do with creation;
• Son – the cross and people figures with arms upraised;

• Holy Spirit – pictures representing a dove, wind and fire.

Paste these on to the background sheet.

USES: *Use to help explain the Trinity – that although there are three separate segments, together they have made one circle. Although each segment is about a separate person, together they make one God. Bring out that each person is interested in and cares about each one of us: the Father who made the world and cares for us; Jesus, his Son, who was once a man, but a very special one; and the Holy Spirit, sent by the Father to help us do what is right.*

USING FABRIC OR PAPER

a Friends of Jesus

From paper or fabric cut a large yellow circle to represent the sun and place it centrally on a dark paper or fabric background. Add rays if desired and the words, 'Jesus is alive. He is our friend'. Children can then contribute to this basic banner either by writing their names, drawing their portraits or adding their handprints. Do writing, drawing, painting, etc, on to paper first, not directly on to banner.

USES: *Link with an Easter theme and a theme on friendship with Jesus. The banner could be kept over a longish period, allowing newcomers to add their contributions and letting the children update what they have done from time to time.*

b Pentecost

Make a banner from beige, brown or green fabric or paper, using markers or fabric pens to write the words, 'The Holy Spirit – God's gift for us'. Decorate with flame designs using yellow, red and orange-coloured fabric or paper.

USES: *Link with the story of Pentecost or Holy Spirit theme and use as a display item.*

c Advent banners

Use fabric, a strip of lining paper or the back of a length of wallpaper to make the banners shown opposite.

USES: *Use leading up to Christmas. If made from fabric, these could be kept from year to year and brought out in the weeks leading up to Christmas. Each one could be covered with a curtain which could be drawn back to reveal one of the pictures week by week – in place of, or linking with, lighting advent candles.*

d Jesus is light

Use card, plain fabric or a length of lining or wallpaper for dark and light backgrounds as required. Cut the letters from brightly-coloured felt or paper and paste on to the background, adding simple pictures of candles or lanterns, etc, as shown below, also cut from fabric, felt or paper. Hang using poles or canes.

USES: *Link with a light theme and Jesus' teaching to do with light.*

• Attach a piece of garden cane to the top and bottom and hang the banner from a length of ribbon.

The promise of a Saviour

revealed in the Bible

• Cut the Bible outline out of felt and add a ribbon bookmark.

The promise of a Saviour

revealed to Mary

• Use fabric pens or marker pens to write the captions.

• Use fabric for the clothes, and felt for hands and feet.

The promise of a Saviour

revealed to the Shepherds

• Use cotton wool and scraps of fabric for the sheep.

The promise of a Saviour

revealed to US

• Give each of the children a circle of card and let them draw their own face. Add wool for the hair.

14 Let's make hats, masks and headbands

COIN HEADDRESS

Follow the illustration to make coin headdresses.

USES: *Link with the parable of the lost coin, also with Jewish wedding customs.*

• Cover a length of card with foil.

• Tape or staple card into a circle to fit child's head.

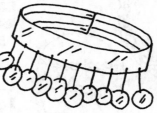

• Attach 10 foil circles/milk bottle tops to front of headband.

'Hello ... Do you like my hat?'
'I do. What a hat!'
'I like it! I like that party hat!'

Lots of hats of all shapes and sizes feature in *Go, Dog. Go!* – one of the beginner books in a reading scheme which features the famous Dr Seuss. Hats, hair and headdresses feature in this section, too, along with headbands and masks – in fact, anything that will fit on the head. Just as children can 'become' someone or something else by talking through a puppet, so they can become someone or something else through putting on a mask, a pair of ears, a headdress, a hat.

Headgear has an enormous potential for enabling children to enter fully into the experience of a story, helping them to feel they are actually there. It is also an ideal way of involving a large number of children – after all, Moses probably had more in his flock than just the first three sheep to raise their hooves! Best of all, none of these items is especially difficult to make. If you haven't tried it before, use shirring elastic on the masks and headbands. It doesn't catch in the hair like a rubber band and is more stretchy and easier to tie than ribbed elastic.

So have a go at making:

FLAME HEADBAND

Follow the directions to make flame headbands. Strips and flames can be pre-cut for younger children, but let them colour in the flame.

USES: *Link with the coming of the Holy Spirit at Pentecost.*

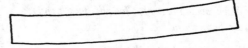

• Cut a strip of paper, 2 cm deep x 56 cm long. Cut out a 'flame' about 10 cm high, colour, and paste to headband.
• Fasten ends together with sticky tape, adjusting length to fit child's head.

SHEEP HEADBANDS	**EGYPTIAN HEADBAND**	**CROWNS**
COIN HEADDRESS	**EGYPTIAN HEADDRESS**	**LEADER'S HAT**
FLAME HEADBAND		**SHEEP MASKS** a Shaped mask b Round masks
TRINITY HEADBANDS	**EGYPTIAN HAIR** **WIGS OR HEADDRESSES**	**COW MASK** **PERSON MASK**

SHEEP HEADBANDS

Make headbands using card and/or shirring elastic as shown.

USES: *Use with stories to do with sheep (eg, Jesus' parables, Moses in the wilderness, themes from minor prophets).*

EWE (ears)   Tape or staple

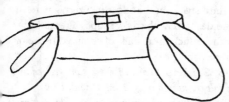

• Cut strip of stiff paper/card and adjust to child's head size using a staple or sticky tape.

RAM (horns)   Shirring elastic

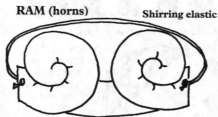

• Alternatively, cut strip to fit the front of the child's head and hold on using shirring elastic. Cut out, colour and paste on horns or ears as preferred.

TRINITY HEADBANDS

Follow the illustration to make headbands from wool or card. A third alternative is to plait together three different colours of used tights or stockings.

USES: *Link with a discussion on the Trinity, pointing out the significance of the three parts and how together they form one.*

Using wool

1. Plait wool.

2. Tie both ends together to fit child's head.

Using card

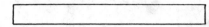

1. Cut strip of card 5–6 cm wide and long enough to fit around child's head.

2. Fold card in half and cut slits.

3. Colour and cut out three narrow strips of card.

4. Weave strips in and out of slits.

EGYPTIAN HAIR

Use a circle or long strip of black crêpe paper cut into a long fringe. Tape the strip into a circle to fit on top of the head. Cut the front fringe shorter as shown.

USES: *Use as for Egyptian items above; different colours with a shorter length could be used in other dressing-up situations.*

WIGS OR HEADDRESSES

Make paper wigs as shown from white paper. These could be made in other colours to serve as headdresses or hats for different occasions. Longer strips flowing down over the shoulders can create a headdress feel.

USES: *Link with a 'courtroom' theme, eg, Peter and John before the Council; use for other dressing-up occasions, eg, for important people instead of the usual 'tea towel' headdress.*

• Cut out a paper bag for the head.

• Curl up strips of paper around a pencil and paste on to the paper hood.

EGYPTIAN HEADBAND

Follow the diagram to make Egyptian headbands.

USES: *Use in helping the children think more deeply about the story of Joseph; link with any Egyptian theme.*

For each band you will need:
1 strip of coloured sugar paper 60 x 3 cm,
2 strips of sugar paper in different colours 60 x 4 cm.

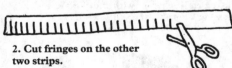

1. Choose one 4 cm strip to be the base colour.

2. Cut fringes on the other two strips.

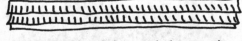

3. Tape the fringed pieces to the base, putting the narrow piece on top.

4. Fit the band to the child's head, trim ends and tape together.

EGYPTIAN HEADDRESS

Make the headdress according to the illustration.

USES: *Use as for Egyptian headband, above.*

You will need:
A large sheet of paper (newsprint or lining paper, 60 x 30 cm),
Scissors,
Blue and yellow paint.

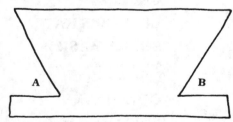

1. Pre-cut the shape as shown.

2. Paint in blue and yellow stripes.

3. When dry, fit A to B round the child's head. Arrange the flap over head.

CROWNS

Make different styles of crowns from silver or gold card. Use coloured foil or cellophane (sweet wrappers) for jewels. Add strips of card as shown opposite and decorate these for a high crown. You could line the inside of this crown with crêpe paper for added effect. For a third style, cut the edges in a zigzag pattern and decorate with sticky shapes alternating with scrunched-up balls of coloured tissue or crêpe paper.

USES: *Link with any theme or story related to royalty or kingship, eg, King David, King Nebuchadnezzar, wise men in Jesus' birth stories; link with the theme of being/feeling important.*

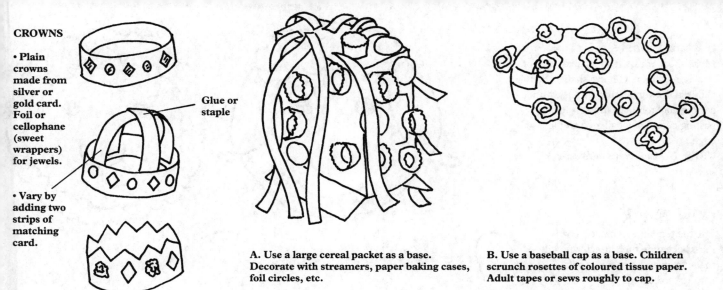

CROWNS

• Plain crowns made from silver or gold card. Foil or cellophane (sweet wrappers) for jewels.

Glue or staple

• Vary by adding two strips of matching card.

A. Use a large cereal packet as a base. Decorate with streamers, paper baking cases, foil circles, etc.

USES: *Use with the theme of leadership. The hat should be worn by those leading various activities, eg, the leader of a game, the one telling a story, the one giving news, the one handing out the biscuits, the leader in 'Follow the leader'.*

B. Use a baseball cap as a base. Children scrunch rosettes of coloured tissue paper. Adult tapes or sews roughly to cap.

LEADER'S HAT

Make hats as shown above. Decorate in any way you choose, the more elaborate the creation, the better, involving as many children as possible in the making of it.

SHEEP MASKS

a Shaped mask

Use the template to make a sheep mask which can be coloured in or pasted and covered with cotton wool. Attach a strip of stiff card or piece of garden cane to the back with sticky tape, to use as a handle to hold up the mask.
USES: *Use with stories featuring sheep.*

b Round masks

Make sheep masks from paper plates or card circles, as shown. Cut eye shapes, then let children draw in features. Finish with a cotton wool forelock and ears, or by pasting cotton wool all around the edge.

USES: *Use with stories to do with sheep.*

COW MASK

Use the template to make a cow mask, decorate then attach a handle made from garden cane or stiff card to the back.

USES: *Use in stories featuring cows to help the children experience the story, eg, Pharaoh's dream, food and drink theme.*

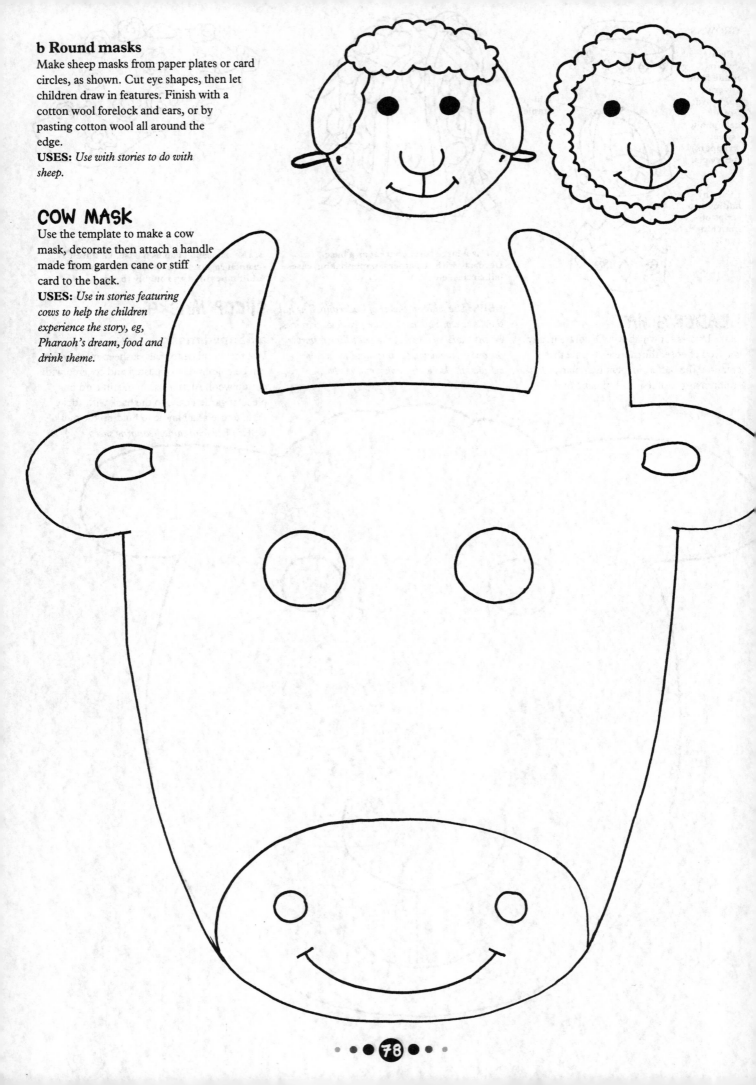

PERSON MASK

Make sad and happy person masks as illustrated.

USES: *Use when telling a story involving a change in the person from being sad to being happy, eg, healing stories such as the paralysed man, Jacob at discovering Joseph was alive, Onesimus when he joined Jesus' family.*

• **Cut two masks from card and cut out eye shapes. Glue wool or strips of paper for hair.**

• **Cut lengths of paper 5 x 3 cm. Roll around a pencil to form tubes for the noses. Glue to masks.**

• **Cut two mouth shapes. Make one mask 'happy'. Make the other 'sad' by inverting the mouth.**

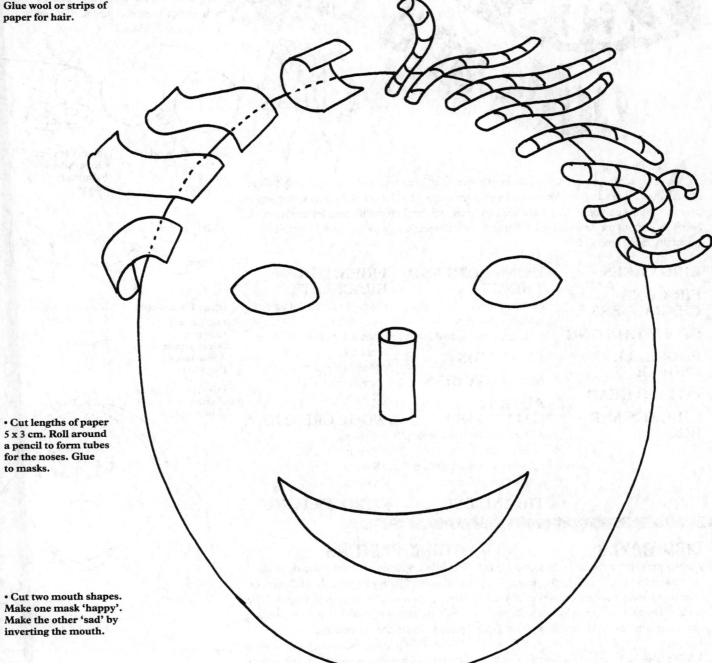

15 Let's make odds and ends

And finally ...

This section covers a miscellaneous selection of items which do not obviously fit into any other category. And as many of them seemed like lots of fun – tie and dye, wool creations, stone painting – they have been grouped together here rather than leaving them out. So if you want to try something just that little bit different, have a look below. Something might just catch your eye!

BIRD CAKES

FIR-CONE CHARACTERS

STONE PAINTING

EGGSHELL PEOPLE

POTATO HEAD

CHICKEN AND EGG

USING POTS AND THINGS
a Make a well
b Make a flowerpot
c Make a hanging basket

PEG BIRDS

MAKING COINS

ADVENT CALENDARS
a Traditional calendar (older children)
b Advent promise calendar (younger children)

TIE AND DYE

FRIENDSHIP BRACELETS
a Wool bracelets (older children)
b Straw bracelets (younger children)
c Ring bracelets (younger children)
d Watch bracelets

WOOL CREATIONS
a Weaving
b Painting
c Sewing
d Collage

CARD WEAVING

option is to fill the eggshell with cotton wool and mustard and cress seeds.
USES: *Link with a theme on growing, or Bible stories to do with planting and reaping, eg, Jesus' story of the man who went out and planted some seeds.*

POTATO HEAD
Use a potato or other firm vegetable as a basis for making a vegetable person. Follow the illustrations for ideas.

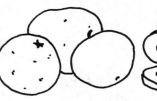

Ideas for heads:
Potatoes
Apples
Oranges

Ideas for eyes:
Carrot slices
Sultanas
Olives

Ideas for mouths and noses:
Cherries
Sweet pepper slices
Apple slices
Bay leaves

Ideas for hair:
Cabbage leaves
Cress
Broccoli

• Use toothpicks or cocktail sticks to join pieces.

BIRD CAKES
Make a present for the birds. Mix cooking fat with bacon rind, currants, apple pieces, cooked potato, oats, cake crumbs and bread scraps. Then fill a coconut half or a plastic container with the 'cake' and hang from a tree branch.
USES: *Link with a theme of caring for God's world; link also with God's care for sparrows and us.*

FIR-CONE CHARACTERS
Provide fir-cones, together with plasticine, glue, seed pods, tiny feathers, pieces of card and so on, and let the children use their imagination to turn the cones into birds, animals or other characters.
USES: *Link with a creativity theme; link with the story of the artisans building the temple.*

STONE PAINTING
Provide large, smooth stones and decorate with paint, felt-tipped pens, dried flowers or small pictures cut from greetings cards. When dry, have an adult varnish them, then paste a piece of felt to the bottom of each pebble.
USES: *Give as gifts, ornaments, paperweights or doorstops, depending on the size. A link could be made with Jacob using a stone as a pillow or with the memorial stones set up after crossing the Jordan.*

EGGSHELL PEOPLE
Draw faces on eggshells, then fill the eggs with soil or potting compost. Stand in prepared 'egg-cups' (an egg-box section pasted on to a piece of card). Sprinkle a little bird seed on top of the soil and water gently. Keep in a warm place and water regularly and watch the 'people' grow green hair. Another

CHICKEN AND EGG
Cut out a chicken and egg. Paste the chick on to the back of the egg with the bottom half of the egg covering all but the chicken's back and head as shown. Attach the top of the egg with *Blu-Tack* so that it can be removed to make the chick 'hatch'.
USES: *Use with a new life theme, linking with the Easter story.*

USING POTS AND THINGS

a Make a well

Decorate a strip of paper with 'stonework' effect and paste the ends of the paper around a yoghurt pot. Ideally, use a yoghurt pot which is not tapered at the bottom. Make holes in opposite sides of the yoghurt pot and make an arch of wire (12 cm). Then push the ends of the wire through the holes in the pot

and use *Blu-Tack* to hold them in place. Make another hole on one side, under the arch, large enough to fit a matchstick. Push the matchstick through the hole and attach a length of string to it. Wind the string around the arch twice and attach the other end to a bottle lid (to act as a bucket) using *Blu-Tack*.
USES: *Link with stories such as Jeremiah in the well, Abraham's servant drawing water from the well, the Samaritan woman.*

b Make a flowerpot

Pierce a few holes in the base of a small plastic pot. Paste enough gummed shapes on the outside of the pot to cover it, or decorate the pot to look like a face. Fill with soil and sow seeds or place a small plant in the pot. Give as a gift.
USES: *Link with a theme on growing things; make as gifts for special occasions.*

c Make a hanging basket

Make hanging baskets using large plastic pots or tubs as shown below.
USES: *These can be given as gifts.*

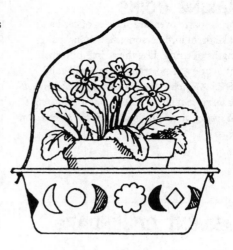

• Pierce a hole in each side of the rim of a margarine tub. Thread string and knot.
• Place small stones in it.
• Decorate the tub with gummed shapes or coloured paper. (Use PVA glue.)
• Add small plants.

PEG BIRDS

Colour, mount on card and cut out bird shapes such as those shown above. Paste the body of the bird to one side of a flat wooden clothes peg. Another option is to use two rectangles of card. On one write 'Messages', and decorate the other with artwork or sticky shapes. Cover both rectangles with clear, sticky-backed plastic and paste to either side of a clothes peg.
USES: *These make good gifts, and, depending on the drawing or wording used, can link with a topical theme.*

MAKING COINS

Spread paste over large circles of card and make them into personalised 'coins' using lengths of string. Use the string to form an initial or a self-portrait (as on a real coin).
USES: *Compare the finished results, linking with the theme that just as all the coins are different but special, so we are all different but all special to Jesus.*

TIE AND DYE

Collect pieces of white or very pale material for dyeing, eg, T-shirts, socks, pillow-cases, handkerchiefs. In an old washing-up bowl or tub, prepare some cold water dye as directed on the packet. Bunch the material concertina-fashion and use broad elastic bands, clothes pegs or string to hold the folds. Gathering up little sections of the material into a pointed shape and securing the material very tightly with a rubber band will produce a sunburst effect. Ensure that the material has been secured tightly enough to prevent the dye permeating into the tied sections.

When tightly bunched, tie a length of string on to one corner of the material and allow the children to dip the material into the prepared dye, then hang up to dry. When dry, allow the children to untie their own items.

Make sure the children are wearing old clothing and are well covered for this activity in case of accidental spills. Also be sure to tell

---

ADVENT CALENDARS

a Traditional calendar (older children)

Draw twenty-five numbered squares on a piece of paper (graph paper is useful here), and cut around three sides of each square to make doors (a craft knife is useful here with supervision). Place this sheet on top of a second sheet of paper, hold in place with paper-clips, then open the doors and draw around the inside edge of each door on to the second sheet. Lift off the first sheet of paper to reveal twenty-five squares. Draw or paste a little Christmas-related picture inside each square (refer to other advent calendars for ideas), then paste the two sheets together around the edges. Close all the doors and decorate the front with glitter, stars, etc.
USES: *Give as a gift or take home and use in the days leading up to Christmas.*

b Advent promise calendar
(younger children)

On four small rectangles of card (one for each Sunday in Advent), write promises or Christmas messages from the Bible, or paste on small Christmas pictures cut from old greetings cards (see illustration). Paste or staple these four cards on to a background ribbon, strip of felt or card. Next make a paper chain of twenty-five links and staple to the top of the ribbon – one for each day of advent. Complete the 'calendar' by adding a nativity picture (drawn or cut from a card) to the top of the ribbon, and a wool tassel to the bottom. Hang with a wool loop.
USES: *Give as gifts or take home and remove one link of the chain each day up to Christmas, beginning on December 1st.*

Wool loop

Ribbon, felt or card

Christmas card scene

Staple chains to ribbon.

He will come again one day

He will hear us when we pray

He will be with us everywhere

He will forgive us if we are sorry

Promise cards – one for each Sunday in Advent – paste to ribbon.

1.

2. Clip   Clip

3.

4. Glitter

Paste

26 links of paper chain, one for each day of Advent.

parents to wash these items separately! NB If this is a new activity for you, be sure to try it out beforehand.

USES: *Use with a theme on colour or on materials; link with the story of the making of the special tent and the coloured materials used in it.*

FRIENDSHIP BRACELETS

a Wool bracelets (older children)

For each child you will need six strands of wool (two each of three colours) 60–70 cm long, starting off with longer than you need (as the wool 'shrinks' when it is knotted). Knot all six threads together at one end, then pair the colours, plait for about 4 cm, then tie a second knot. (At this point attach the bracelet with a safety-pin to your belt, jeans or a soft object leaving both hands free to knot the wool.) Now begin to make knots with the wool as shown in the illustration. Each set of knots should bring a new stripe of colour into the bracelet.

b Straw bracelets (younger children)

Cut plenty of 'beads' – small sections of coloured drinking straws – for threading on to a length of wool to form a bracelet. Tie the first section of straw on to the bottom end of the wool and wrap a strip of sticky tape tightly around the other end of the wool to make a 'needle'.

c Ring bracelets (younger children)

Cut rings from the cylinders of washing-up liquid containers. Decorate with paste and sticky shapes of coloured paper, or with permanent spirit-based markers (with supervision).

d Watch bracelets

Prepare strips of strong but flexible card, 20 x 3 cm. Decorate as desired. Draw watch faces on small circles of card (or a decorative pattern), and paste on to the centre of the strips. Fasten by slotting the two cuts together (see illustration).

Cut

Cut

USES for friendship bracelets: *Link with a theme on friendship and loyalty, eg, David and Jonathan; these can be given as gifts to a special friend or family member.*

WOOL BRACELET

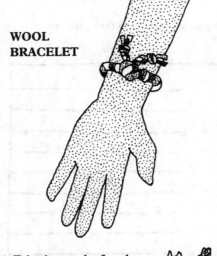

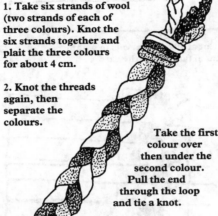

1. Take six strands of wool (two strands of each of three colours). Knot the six strands together and plait the three colours for about 4 cm.

2. Knot the threads again, then separate the colours.

Take the first colour over then under the second colour. Pull the end through the loop and tie a knot.

3. Do this twice. In the same way use the first colour to tie two knots on the third colour. The first colour now lies in third place.

4. Now use the second colour to tie knots on the third, then the first colour. Repeat the process with the third colour.

Continue in this way until the bracelet is long enough to go around the child's wrist.

5. Tie another knot in the six strands of wool. Plait a further 4 cm and then tie a final knot. Use the plaited sections to tie the bracelets around the child's wrist.

WOOL CREATIONS

a Weaving

Join a length of wool to a forked twig and weave the wool in and out around the twig, tying on a new colour of wool to the old end when the previous colour is finished.

b Painting

Prepare short lengths of thick wool gripped in clothes pegs. Dip the wool into paint and draw it across paper to create a design.

c Sewing

Provide blunt darning needles threaded with brightly coloured wool for 'sewing' through a piece of net bag (in which fruit is sold), a polystyrene tray, or a piece of card (as shown below).

You will need:
Piece of card,
Wool,
Blunt needle,
Hole punch.

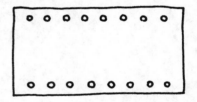

1. Punch holes along opposite edges of the card.

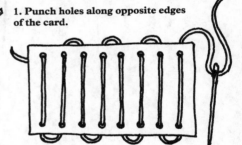

2. Sew on bars using either wool and a blunt needle, or wool with taped ends.

d Collage

Provide thin coloured card, lengths of wool in different colours and paste to create collage work.

USES for wool creations: *Link with stories to do with sheep; link with the theme of caring and protection, paralleling how the shepherd cares for his sheep with how God cares for us; link with a materials theme, eg, wool.*

CARD WEAVING

Make mats by weaving card as shown.

USES: *Link with a theme on materials, also with stories of the woven materials prepared for the tent of meeting.*

Prepare coloured card for each child.

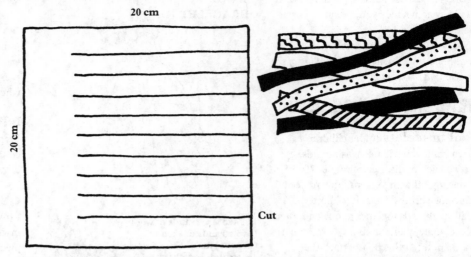

20 cm

20 cm

Cut

1. Cut at 20 cm intervals to within 4 cm of far edge of the card.

2. Provide 6 different coloured strips of card measuring 2 cm by 22 cm.

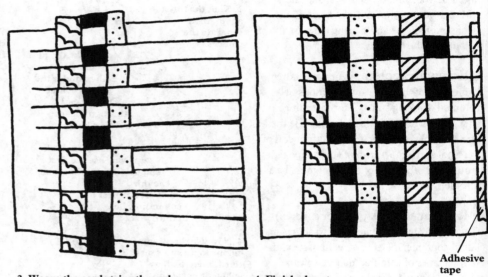

3. Weave the card strips through. When finished, seal the edge with adhesive tape.

4. Finished mat.

Adhesive tape

16 Let's make templates

In this section, you will find a variety of useful templates which can be used in conjunction with many of the ideas suggested in the book. In addition to animal and people outlines, you will also find a number of geometric shapes such as a circle, an oval, a star and so on, as well as a few Christmas shapes. Each of these may be photocopied, enlarged or reduced. They can be cut out and used as stencils; coloured in and used in pictures and friezes; pasted and covered with collage material; written on, cut out and hung up in mobiles; folded and used to make cards ... In short, they can be VERY USEFUL. Have fun using them!

PEOPLE

FRUIT

ANIMALS (FARM AND WILD)

WEATHER SYMBOLS

CHRISTMAS SHAPES

GEOMETRIC SHAPES

PEOPLE

FRUIT

FRUIT

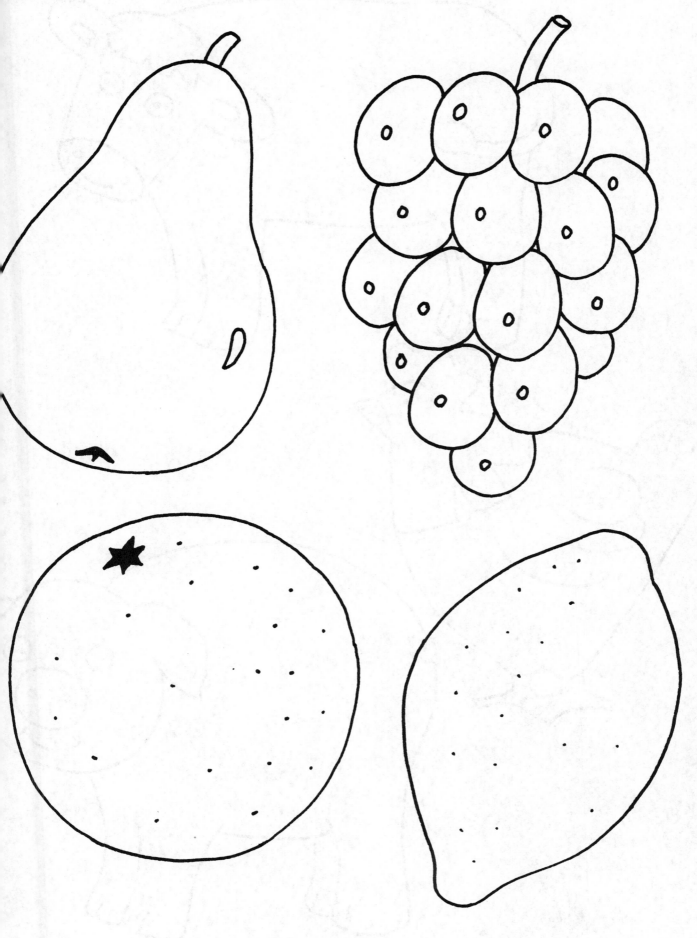

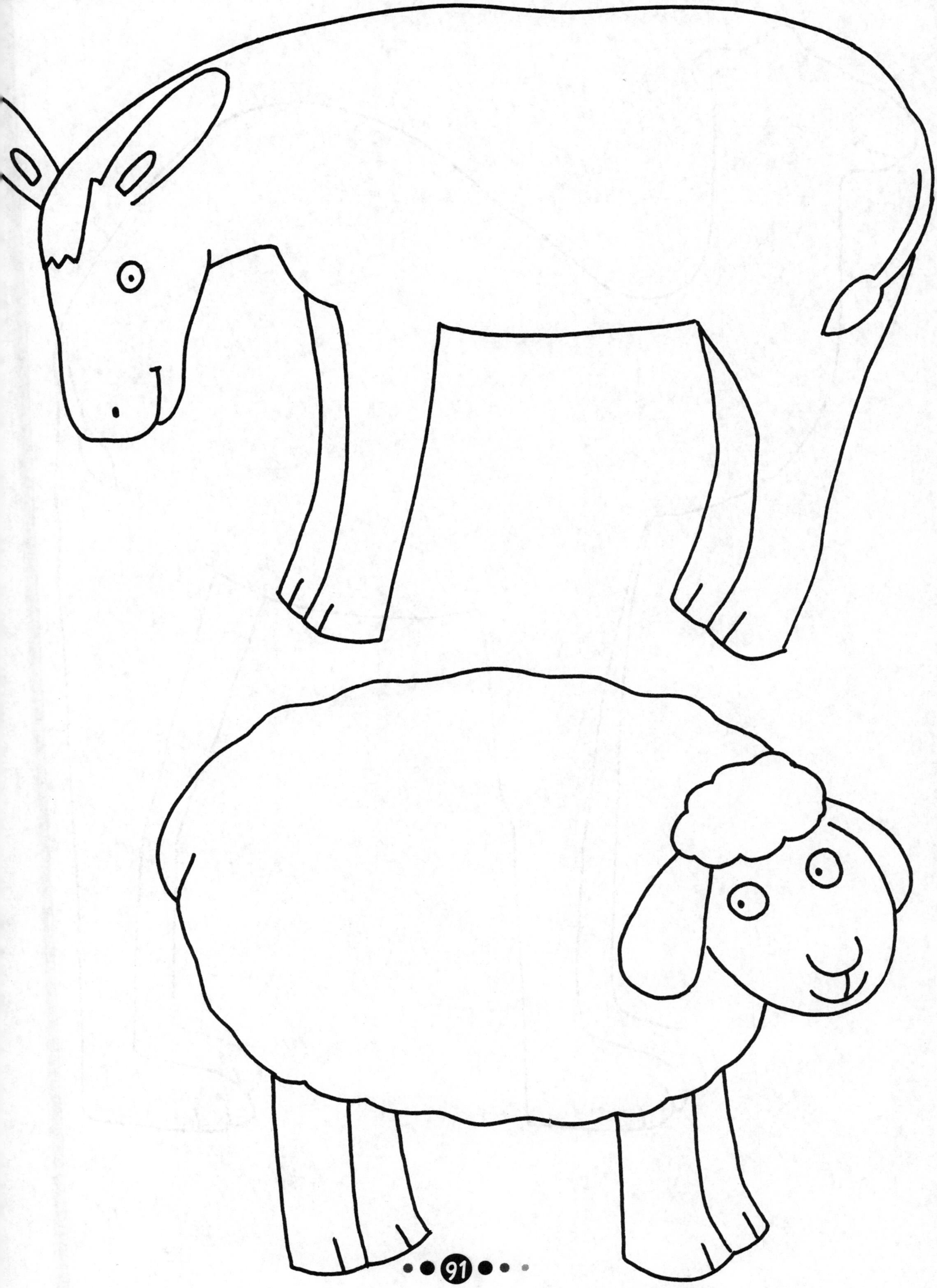

WEATHER SYMBOLS

CHRISTMAS SHAPES

GEOMETRIC SHAPES

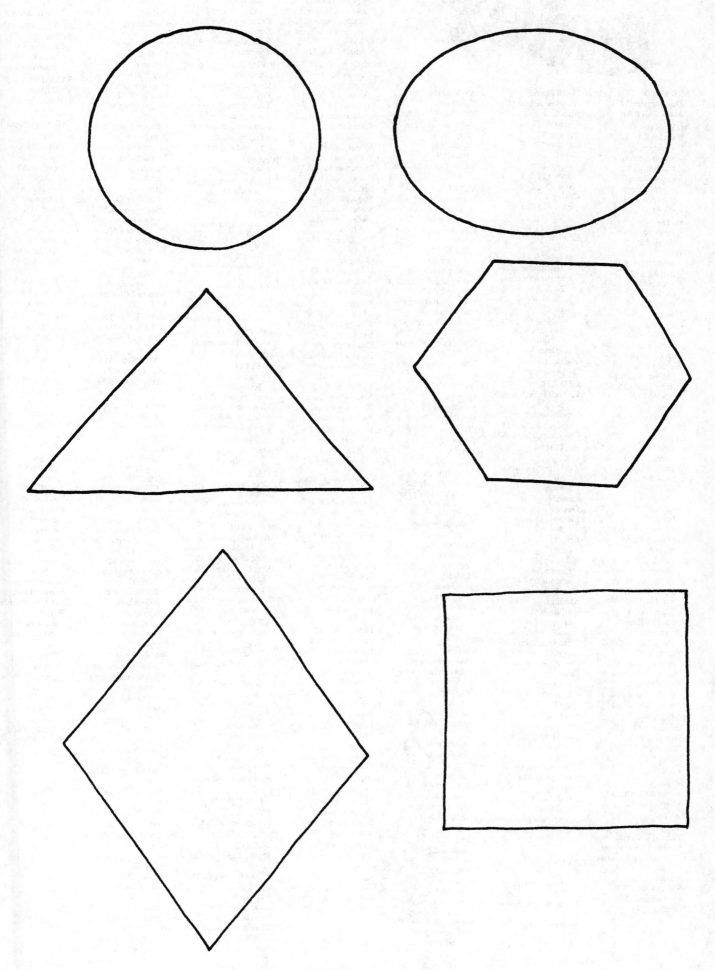